Praise for *The Prepared Leader*

"*The Prepared Leader* is a strong roadmap for how to lead during a crisis, filled with relatable, real-world examples. I found myself nodding my head and saying 'yes' while reading. The book also inspires us all and reminds us that with preparation, companies and their team members can emerge from challenging times stronger and more resilient than ever, and spawning a new phase of innovation."
—**Roz Brewer, Chief Executive Officer, Walgreens Boots Alliance**

"Brilliant and fast-reading, *The Prepared Leader*, by Erika H. James and Lynn Perry Wooten, is a must-read for anyone who aspires to successfully navigate a major crisis—for the sake of their organization, their employees, and their customers. Their research supports what I've experienced leading a company in a time of crisis: developing the right skills, continuing to learn, and leveraging the power of a diverse and knowledgeable team are all essential aspects of becoming a Prepared Leader."
—**Ed Bastian, CEO, Delta Air Lines**

"*The Prepared Leader* is a timely assessment of what it takes to be an effective leader in our hyper-connected world. In detailing how best to identify and plan for a crisis of any size, Erika H. James and Lynn Perry Wooten provide an informed strategy any executive can employ. However, by including thoughtful methods for learning from our challenges, James and Wooten ensure every reader can take away invaluable lessons to prepare us for an unknown future."
—**James Gorman, Chairman and CEO, Morgan Stanley**

"The best leaders both anticipate areas where a crisis might emerge, and they prepare themselves and their teams to respond. *The Prepared Leader*, by Erika H. James and Lynn Perry Wooten, is an excellent playbook for doing both. The frameworks and processes they share are world-class."
—**Reggie Fils-Aime, Former President and COO of Nintendo of America, and Author, *Disrupting the Game: From the Bronx to the Top of Nintendo***

"*The Prepared Leader* was written for this moment—but it stems from years of research and the personal experience of two remarkable and pathbreaking leaders. . . . Wooten and James have written this book for all of us who lead organizations, teams, and enterprises in an exceedingly complicated world."
—**Judy Samuelson, Executive Director, Aspen Institute Business & Society Program**

"This book is truly special and right on time. In their important new book, Erika H. James and Lynn Perry Wooten provide aspiring and established leaders with a roadmap for navigating competing crises such as racial injustice, political upheaval, economic instability, and pandemic recovery. For leaders of organizations fighting and advocating for societal change, *The Prepared Leader* is an essential read, revealing how we can shape better outcomes. This book is a must read."
—**Wes Moore, Bestselling Author and Former CEO, Robin Hood Foundation**

"Erika James and Lynn Wooten have created a guidebook for those who know we need to be a Prepared Leader. . . . We probably won't know exactly what the next crisis will be, but we can be prepared. With real world examples of leaders who flourished in the crisis of COVID to those who failed spectacularly in the tectonic shift in racial justice, every chapter has something to teach us."
—**Karen Finerman, CEO & Co-founder, Metropolitan Capital Advisors**

"Erika H. James and Lynn Perry Wooten present a practical and insightful tour through the critical elements of effective crisis management. . . . James and Wooten show that crises provide risks coupled with opportunities and that the leaders who thrive during crises are those who push themselves to learn thoroughly and rapidly and to seize on both wins and losses."
—**Ruth Porat, SVP & Chief Financial Officer, Alphabet and Google**

"In my experience, crises are inevitable; the question is how you respond. In their well-researched and actionable new book, *The Prepared Leader*, Erika H. James and Lynn Perry Wooten share the stories of the companies that have successfully navigated crises and offer guidance to help organizations prepare for and manage through uncertain times and challenging moments."
—**Vikram Malhotra, Senior Partner, McKinsey & Company, and Chair, Wharton Graduate Executive Board**

"Erika H. James and Lynn Perry Wooten's *The Prepared Leader* . . . offers a wealth of insights and best practices that empower managers at any level to successfully navigate whatever crisis comes their way. A must-read for managing the unexpected in an ever more complex and interconnected world."
—**Alex Gorsky, Executive Chairman, Johnson & Johnson**

"Dean James and President Wooten have penned an indisputable blueprint of how to successfully manage, leverage, and emerge victoriously from any global crisis. More importantly, they invite leaders to be deeply introspective to challenge themselves to an elevated level of leadership."
—**Carla Harris, Senior Client Advisor, Morgan Stanley, and Author, *Lead to Win and Expect to Win***

"Erika H. James and Lynn Perry Wooten have written a brilliant new book, *The Prepared Leader*. They lay out a practical framework to help leaders build teams, manage through crises, and help their institutions emerge even stronger. I only wish the book had been available as we navigated the Great Financial Crisis!"
—**F. William (Bill) McNabb III, Former Chairman and CEO, Vanguard Group**

"Combining extensive experience and evidence, this dynamic duo has created the road map you need to prepare for the unexpected."
—**Adam Grant, "10 Books to Enrich Your Thinking"; Wharton School professor and bestselling author, *Think Again***

ERIKA H.
JAMES

LYNN PERRY
WOOTEN

THE
PREPARED
LEADER

EMERGE FROM ANY CRISIS
MORE RESILIENT THAN BEFORE

WHARTON
SCHOOL
PRESS
Philadelphia

Published by Wharton School Press
The Wharton School
University of Pennsylvania
3620 Locust Walk
300 Steinberg Hall-Dietrich Hall
Philadelphia, PA 19104
Email: whartonschoolpress@wharton.upenn.edu
Website: wsp.wharton.upenn.edu

Ebook ISBN: 9781613631621
Paperback ISBN: 9781613631638
Hardcover ISBN: 9781613631652
Institutional Edition ISBN: 9781613631676

We dedicate this book to our mothers, Gloria Hayes Rosenberg and Deloris Stallings Perry, who nurtured and prepared us for leadership; to our husbands, Jimmie E. James and David B. Wooten, whose love and support sustains us; and to our children, Jordan James, Alexandra James, Justin Wooten, and Jada Wooten, for inspiring us to prepare the next generation of leaders.

Contents

Introduction

From late 2019 into early 2020, we each faced extraordinary professional and personal challenges—and opportunities. Erika was in talks with The Wharton School of the University of Pennsylvania to become its next dean. She would become the first woman and the first person of color to hold that role in the school's more than 130-year history. At the same time, Lynn had been appointed president of Simmons University, one of the most progressive institutions in the United States, with a long, storied tradition of advancing social justice. Lynn, too, was about to become the first African American leader of a historic American university.

The stakes felt incredibly high. For both of us, these leadership roles came with huge responsibility. We would be very much in the public eye and prone to public scrutiny. Our experience as leaders would be put to the test in altogether new ways, as daunting as they were exciting. We anticipated this responsibility and the curiosity that our appointments would arouse—the many eyes within our organizations, our industry, and the academic community, watching and evaluating our decisions and choices in the months ahead.

And we had questions of our own to ponder: How would we safeguard the integrity, the quintessential caliber of these great institutions, while also making a difference? How would we build the knowledge and understanding, as well as the relationships and trust, to forge new commitments and a new vision to drive progress for the future? How would we do our very best by our staff, our faculty, and our communities of learners, ensuring they would have what they need to lead for tomorrow's opportunities?

These were the questions in front of us. They were timely, but they weren't altogether new.

Although it was a coincidence for us to find ourselves facing these questions at the same juncture in our lives and careers and at the same moment in time, it wasn't altogether surprising either.

For more than 25 years, our lives have been linked and intertwined in many ways. We first met in a statistics class at the University of Michigan, both hungry learners working on our PhDs. Back then, we were struck by the commonalities in our thinking. We found exciting common ground in the things that truly kindled our curiosity—ideas that simply demanded to be understood better. These concepts were largely tied to leadership—the practice of leadership and its agency and the power leaders have to create positive change, or its opposite. We also shared an interest in, as well as lived experience of, the myriad, complex issues involved in discrimination, diversity, and inclusion.

Diversity went on to become the primary focus of our joint research, and in 2006 we published a paper that looked at the effects of race discrimination lawsuits filed against Texaco leadership and the ensuing damage to its organizational reputation. This was our entrée into the study of crises and crisis management.

Here began a body of work that has addressed other critical questions: Why does one organization or leader thrive in extreme difficulty or pressure, whereas others flounder? And what are the aptitudes and capabilities, and the attitudes and mindsets, that make certain people successful (or not) when the chips are down? We have continued to explore crises themselves: what they are, how they unfold over time, and what they mean in terms of opportunity as well as threat.

We have worked together as researchers, collaborators, coauthors, and friends to give full rein to the interests that we share. Together we've studied, taught, and consulted on many aspects of leadership and crisis management. We've looked at natural and national disasters, simmering and sudden crises, and the pervasive and pernicious impact of discrimination on the workforce and on organizational reputation. We've published papers on Martha Stewart, #MeToo, and campus crises, on Emory's health-care systems and Ebola, and on Hurricane Katrina and 9/11.

During these many years, our personal and professional trajectories have run broadly in parallel. We have both had the privilege to teach students, executives, and leaders at some of the most interesting and dynamic organizations in the United States. We have been fortunate to lead world-class departments, teams, and institutions. We have had unique and exciting opportunities to enact many of the findings of our research in situ, in our leadership practice, and within historic and renowned institutions. Between us, we have a combined 30 years of research, teaching, and leadership in several highly prestigious schools. Before Simmons, Lynn was at Cornell University as the David J. Nolan Dean and Professor of Management and Organizations at the Dyson School of Applied Economics and Management. Erika enjoyed a six-year tenure as dean of Emory University's Goizueta Business School before taking the helm at Wharton. We've put together much of our most important research and insights on our website, https://jamesandwooten.com/.

A Challenge Unlike Any Other

Making the transition to our new leadership roles as 2020 began, the challenge before us was still extraordinary. It was a challenge to distill many years of experience, leadership, and research, and put it to work in the service of these historic institutions. It was daunting; it was exciting; and it was an honor. It was personal as well as professional. We were both acutely aware of the responsibilities, the scrutiny, and the difficulties that lay in wait. But we were ready to forge ahead.

Then COVID-19 hit. And the challenge was instantaneously transformed into something far greater than either of us had imagined.

Anyone leading a team or organization in 2020 will know how extraordinarily difficult this crisis was to navigate. Anyone who stepped up to new responsibilities in 2020 will also understand the way COVID-19 put leadership to the test in wholly different ways.

For us, leading Wharton and Simmons through this crisis meant surfacing critical information from multiple sources; building an understanding of our organizational structure, needs, vulnerabilities, and strengths; identifying urgent problems; making crucial and sometimes controversial decisions; and creating the consensus and resources to execute them. And it meant doing all of this incredibly fast, under huge pressure and uncertainty, and in total physical isolation.

But that's not all—because in crises, people look to leaders for emotional intelligence, guidance, and reassurance too. For us this meant establishing new relationships; building bidirectional trust; getting different and diverse people on board; and ensuring they were committed, confident, and resilient enough to align around a plan of action, even as the situation changed day by day, hour by hour. And it meant doing all of this without actually meeting in person.

Why We Wrote This Book

The challenges we thought we were facing multiplied a hundredfold. But so too did the *opportunities*.

If there's one thing we have learned about crises in our research over the years, it is that they bring opportunities as much as they bring risks. Crises are opportunities to sharpen your leadership skills and to unearth new expertise—often in surprising places. They are also opportunities to learn—to determine which important lessons a crisis has to share and to embed those lessons in your leadership practice going forward.

The lessons of the pandemic are manifold and crucial because this was a global event of such magnitude and immediacy—one that was experienced simultaneously by people all over the world. COVID-19 was a singular moment in time—a crisis so unlike any other in living memory that its lessons demand to be explored, understood, and embedded.

As scholars of crisis and crisis management, we understood this imperative even as we were living and experiencing the pandemic in real time, in our jobs and our lives. In fact, however, we had already begun to talk about a new framing around crisis management even before COVID-19 struck. We had started thinking more deeply about the power and instrumentality of leadership before, during, and after crises and about new and better ways to rationalize what we meant in terms of crisis *leadership*.

In particular, we have been investigating the kinds of systemic or cultural failures that create a smoldering crisis: how a lack of diversity and inclusion or a certain organizational myopia can spell disaster down the road. We have also thought deeply about the skills and the attitudes that we believe leaders should enact at each phase of their crisis management, and how learning—or failure to learn—will determine how they weather any storm.

Two ideas have taken deep hold over time. One is that crises are never one-off events. They happen again and again, although we never seem to expect them. The second idea is really the core idea that we want to set out in this book. Because we know that crises happen, how they happen, and that they happen again and again, there is in fact something we can do to manage them. We can *prepare* for them. We can *prepare* our leadership, our organizations, our systems, and our processes to withstand crises, whatever they are, whenever they strike. We can become Prepared Leaders.

Writing *The Prepared Leader* while transitioning into prominent new roles—taking the helm in large organizations and managing new teams while navigating the daily vagaries of this crisis—has been a vast challenge. As much as anything, it has been a challenge to both of us to *walk the talk*: to enact the very ideas we talk about in this book and to dedicate the time to reflect on the learnings from our own leadership practice.

But writing this book has also been cathartic in the sense that it has given us the space to think and reflect deeply about our 30 years of research and their intersection with our lived experience as leaders.

In a crisis, it's all too easy to get caught up in the weeds and forget that you also must lead the strategy of your organization. Effective crisis leadership is about dealing with urgent and immediate needs without ever losing sight of your long-term objectives. To do that, you also must know when to stop, when to step away, and when to make the conscious and cognitive effort to see the bigger picture. Writing this book has been a timely reminder of this need as well as an exercise in servicing it.

Above all, writing this book has given us a chance to do what is essentially part of our DNA as educators: to help develop empowered leaders.

Our goal in writing *The Prepared Leader* is to help you prepare yourself, your teams, your people, and your organization for the next crisis that lies ahead.

We want you to understand the need to prepare *now* and to start putting into place the necessary systems, protocols, and resources. We want you to start scanning your environment, to identify the signs when crisis is imminent, and to build the resilience you need to deflect or contain the damage. We want you to make better decisions when the chips are down and to spot the opportunities, even during a crisis, for recovery and growth. We want you to understand that no one person can do any of this alone and that to truly thrive under pressure, you need the right team, the expertise, and the trust in place, to always see the bigger picture. And we want you to grasp the importance of learning and to convert failure into opportunities to learn—and to build your resilience for the crisis that lies in wait after this. And we want you to start doing all of this now, before that next crisis hits.

This is what a Prepared Leader does.

In the chapters that follow, we set out findings from our own research, alongside stories, recent business cases, and exclusive interviews with leaders and colleagues from different organizations and industries, that illustrate different aspects of Prepared Leadership.

We also share several tools and frameworks as well as key takeaways that you can enact today in your own organization and in your leadership.

In **Chapter 1**, we look at why we were so unprepared for the COVID-19 crisis and the psychology that drives what we refer to as "the cycle of panic and neglect," leaving us vulnerable to shock. We explain how Prepared Leadership breaks this cycle and why being prepared needs to be your "fourth bottom line."

Chapters 2 and 3 take us through the five phases of crisis management and the specific skills and aptitudes we believe you should prioritize as a Prepared Leader to better lead your teams and organization during each phase.

Once we have established this temporal framework, we look at the mechanics of decision-making in **Chapter 4** and see how they come under threat when we experience stress. You discover techniques to help you *prepare and protect* your decision-making, including four critical questions you need to ask yourself.

Chapters 5 and 6 explore how to build and optimize your crisis management team. Here we think about the ways that information flows around your team and your business, and we discuss how Prepared Leaders spot and *defer to* expertise—wherever they find it. We also look at the dynamics at play when you inherit an existing team mid-crisis, as we did. We hear from Mark Turner of the UK's National Health System. We also talk to Wonya Lucas, president and CEO of Crown Media, whose experience of walking in "mid-movie" mirrors our own.

Chapter 7 looks at how crises can become globalized and what it means to have a global mindset as a Prepared Leader. We also look at the *mega communities* of stakeholders who can influence the outcomes of crises and what you can do to empower mega communities of response within your own organization when a crisis strikes.

In **Chapter 8**, we look at technology as a tool to manage crises. We also look at how one disruptive new venture is using technology to preempt crises relating to climate change.

Chapter 9 focuses on learning, the core of Prepared Leadership. We ask why it's so hard for some organizations to learn the lessons of crises and we underscore the importance of doing so. We also share insights and recommendations that you can put into action to drive a learning orientation in your organization.

Finally, we ask, what's next? We talk about our personal experience of the COVID-19 pandemic and what it taught us about Prepared Leadership in terms of our own leadership practice—and what this means for us and for you, as a Prepared Leader, going forward.

In each of the chapters that follow, we articulate the attitudes and behaviors that we believe will empower you to prepare your organization for the difficult times ahead, to contain crises when they occur, and to leverage crises to drive organizational change and unlock future innovation.'

We hope to convince you that being a Prepared Leader isn't as simple as expecting the worst. Being a Prepared Leader is about being optimistic and open to new experiences. It's about having a willingness to learn and take risks, and assuming that all things are possible. Prepared Leadership is the belief that even in times of crisis, people and organizations can emerge more resilient, stronger, and better than they were before.

Chapter 1

Prepared Leadership as Your Fourth Bottom Line

For too long, we have allowed a cycle of panic and neglect when it comes to pandemics: we ramp up efforts when there's a serious threat, then quickly forget about them when the threat subsides.
—Jim Yong Kim, former president, World Bank

On March 11, 2020, Tedros Adhanom Ghebreyesus, the director-general of the World Health Organization (WHO), made an announcement. Cases of the novel coronavirus had recently increased 13-fold, and the spread was set to grow exponentially. COVID-19 had become a pandemic.

Pandemic was not a word the WHO took lightly, Ghebreyesus said. Indeed, so serious was the threat of COVID-19 that "urgent and aggressive" measures were now necessary to contain the virus. "We have rung the alarm bell," he added, "loud and clear."[1]

The WHO was not wrong in its assessment of the threat. Nor was it wrong to ring the alarm bell.

It is all but impossible to fully understand the enormity of the cost of COVID-19 and the other related, interconnected crises that characterize the pandemic era: the social and racial reckoning, the spikes in international tensions, the upswing in protectionism and populism, the so-called Great Resignation, and the intense economic uncertainty of this time.

Some, like the Brookings Institution, have sought to quantify the essentially unquantifiable. In a paper published in 2021, Brookings scholars posited a theoretical dollar value on human life lost to the pandemic at around 17% of global GDP.[2] That is roughly the same in monetary value as the entire Chinese economy at the start of 2019.

The World Bank and others talked about a contraction of 3.4% in the global economy in 2020, with all the world's economies experiencing recession during that year—and emerging markets hit the worst. More than 100 million people were tipped into extreme poverty by 2021, they said.[3]

Meanwhile, government aid packages like the CARES Act in the United States provided emergency buffers for businesses and households around the world but incurred unprecedented sovereign debt, stymying the longer-term outlook for recovery.

And then there is the cost in terms of human capital. Education was one of the biggest losers during the pandemic. School and campus closures kept more than 1.6 billion students out of classrooms at the pandemic's peak, with low-income countries again bearing the brunt. Some economists estimate the cost of lifetime loss in labor earnings for this generation could amount to $12 trillion. Meanwhile, as jobs and firms fell victim to COVID-19, unemployment spiked all over the world. Estimates put the loss in labor income during 2020 at a staggering $3.7 trillion, with young people, the self-employed, blue-collar workers, and women being the hardest hit.[4]

We can only speculate about the other costs of COVID-19: the cost of undiagnosed and untreated illnesses and the longer-term psychological fallout of stay-at-home measures and social distancing. We can't say for sure what the total cost of the pandemic era was for countries, communities, businesses, organizations, households, minority groups, men, women, and children.

What we do know for sure is this: The world was *unprepared*.

A Wake-Up Call for Global Health?

By the time the WHO sounded the alarm bell loud and clear in March 2020, it was probably too late to take anything other than reactive emergency measures to try to contain the damage.

But we had been warned about this crisis earlier. Much earlier.

Back in the 1980s, scientists and epidemiologists, including the Nobel Laureate Joshua Lederberg, had sounded the alarm. Writing in the midst of the AIDS epidemic, Lederberg had this to say: "We will face similar catastrophes again, and will be ever more confounded in dealing with them."[5]

In 1990, journalist Robin Marantz Henig warned about new, potentially devastating pathogens linked to climate change and mass urbanization. Our proximity to farm or forest animals was a huge threat, she said, even as we continued "blithely going about our business."[6]

We even have actual lived experience of other zoonotic viral outbreaks in recent years. The SARS outbreak of early 2000 prompted panic in Beijing and Southeast Asia. A full 20 years ago, quarantines, mask wearing, randomized temperature checks, virtual schoolrooms, and stockpiling of household basics were the norm from Hong Kong to Seoul, to Singapore, to Tokyo—all of it beamed into the global consciousness via headlines from North to West, from the Americas to Europe and beyond. The *Washington Post* ran regular updates describing the virus's "alarming versatility." At the height of this outbreak, *Newsweek* asked its readers: "SARS, can it be stopped?" Meanwhile, the *New York Times* ran a lead opinion piece describing the virus as a "wake-up call for global health."[7]

As recently as 2015, another viral outbreak began to make headlines. Ebola was rarer than SARS but several times more deadly, with an average fatality rate of 50%. Between 2014 and 2016, Ebola spread across six countries in West Africa, killing more than 11,000 people and spreading panic across the globe.

On April 3 that year, Microsoft founder Bill Gates gave a TED talk that garnered tens of millions of online views. In that talk he spoke about the "inevitability" of another pandemic. Viral disease, he said, represented an existential threat to human life far greater than war or nuclear weapons. Gates called on governments around the world to take immediate action and to ramp up preventive measures and protocols ahead of the next global health crisis. In an opinion piece for the *New York Times* that same year, he added: "We know the cost of failing to act." According to the World Bank, a worldwide flu epidemic would reduce global wealth by $3 trillion, not to mention the immeasurable misery caused by millions of deaths.[8]

We began this chapter by saying that it's hard to calculate the total cost of the crises caused by the pandemic. Gates was certainly right about the immeasurability of misery. But he was wrong about the awful enormity of its economic and financial repercussions. His estimates don't even come close.

So, what went wrong?

The Cycle of Panic and Neglect

In 2017, the World Bank's then-president Kim was asked to speak at the opening session of philanthropist Jeff Skoll's World Forum. He had bad news to share. International support for the World Bank's pandemic financing facility had effectively collapsed: Only two active donors were still on board.

This spoke to a pattern Kim had observed during his leadership. Immediately after a crisis, he said, there was a lull—a sudden drop-off in vigilance and caution across the international community that he described as "scary." And it happened every time. Whenever a pandemic hit, the world's leaders responded with alarm. As soon as it was over, the world immediately relaxed. Kim had a description for this behavior. He called it a "cycle of panic, neglect, panic, neglect."[9]

We believe that Kim perfectly captured the dynamic of what happens when human beings deal with things that are sudden, anomalous, and potentially devastating.

When the WHO sounded the alarm on March 11, 2020, COVID was already a full-fledged crisis. And even though the signs had been pointed out, alarm bells had been issued, and we had actually lived through previous viral outbreaks in recent memory, we had stopped thinking about them. Over a relatively short period of time, we allowed our critical surveillance and response mechanisms to atrophy. When COVID-19 hit, we'd dropped the ball, we'd dropped our guard, and we were unprepared. We were victims of the cycle of panic and neglect.

Why Don't We See Crises Coming?

Crises are not the same as routine challenges or problems. They are anomalies. They are atypical events. They don't happen every day. And unlike business problems, crises are hard to resolve using the standard resources or intellectual capabilities that we deploy in the day-to-day.

A crisis can feel like it hits you and your organization out of the blue. In reality, certain types of crises can simmer in the background until the conditions are just right for disaster to materialize. These smoldering crises can be hard to predict, even if they are technically foreseeable. And that's because they are often tied to failure in organizational culture or procedures—the same failure that allows them to happen while also making them hard to see or track. Smoldering crises include things like IT failures or oil spills, as well as weaknesses in organizational culture that allow malpractice, fraud, discrimination, or sexual harassment to take root.

Other types of crises can be genuinely harder to predict. It's tough, for instance, to accurately foresee and plan for events such as natural disasters, terrorist attacks, fires, floods, earthquakes, or pandemics— although, as we explore in this book, it is not impossible.

Unlike business problems, crises are *always* serious. And they always have the potential to wreak havoc on your organization and your stakeholders—your employees, customers, extended communities, and environment. Whether it's COVID-19 or a financial crisis, localized or globalized, sudden or slow-burning, crises are always significant.

They are also inevitable. History, recent evidence, and logic itself tell us that crises always happen. Let's say that again: Crises always happen.

Crises are not one-off events. They happen time and time again. Just as one crisis starts to resolve, another is already taking shape. Unfortunately, human beings are not ideally equipped to rationalize threats like this. We do not ordinarily plan for the atypical, the anomalous, the irregular, or the exceptional on a day-to-day basis. We are hardwired to neglect the possibility of a crisis.

Research in behavioral science and psychology has shed a great deal of light on the way human beings think. We have certain beliefs or cognitive biases that shape the way we understand risks and our response to them. And although these biases are helpful to us in the management of our routines and our day-to-day leadership, they make it very hard for us to foresee disasters, take preemptive actions, make rational decisions under stress, or shift direction when something devastating and frightening happens—even when logic dictates we should.[10]

Let's quickly summarize these cognitive biases in the context of the COVID-19 crisis. And think about them too in the broader, everyday context of how you personally evaluate threats. As you read on, ask yourself: Do these things resonate with you and your leadership?

Probability Neglect: Underrating Bad Outcomes

This is our tendency to underestimate the probability that something (bad) will happen to us.

When Europeans or Americans first heard about the coronavirus outbreak in Wuhan, China, it's likely that many thought it was too far away to be relevant. If leaders were slow to react to the threat of COVID-19, it is probably because many of us doubted it would reach our own shores. And even if it did, they thought it wouldn't spread as fast as it did.

Hyperbolic Discounting: Focusing on the Present over the Future

Humans tend to focus on the present much more than the future. We think about the needs of today far more than those of tomorrow.

This may have helped our ancestors fend off the immediate threat of other predators, but it makes it hard to fully assess potential risks unless they are right in front of us.

Hyperbolic discounting would have made it hard to think about how COVID-19 might affect us and to take preventive measures to minimize the threat and contain damage.

Anchoring Effect: Our First Impression Sinks In

Humans also tend to cleave to the first impression or understanding we form about a risk or threat. The way we initially frame that threat tends to stick—we anchor ourselves to it. If the situation changes, it's very hard for us to shift or adapt our thinking fast enough to keep up with the evolving risks. For instance, even as the international spread of COVID-19 gathered momentum, it was hard to shake off the notion that this was still "someone else's problem."

Exponential Growth Bias: Not Everything Is Straightforward

Most of us struggle to imagine how a situation might evolve or grow in anything other than a straightforward, linear fashion. But the pandemic expanded outward in multiple directions, simultaneously and exponentially—its tentacles quickly encircling people, organizations, communities, industries, and economies all over the world. The speed and multifaceted nature of this spread was hard to make sense of, making it harder still to plan for and respond to quickly and effectively.

Sunk-Cost Fallacy: It's Hard to Change Course

Once we have settled on a course of action, and invested time, effort, and resources, it's hard to change direction. We tend to hang on to an idea or strategy long after the point that it's no longer useful. The

United Kingdom, for instance, came under fire from some parts of the press in 2020 for pursuing what was seen as a herd-immunity strategy at the start of the pandemic. The country later abandoned that strategy, but only months after the first cases had been detected there and several weeks after its neighboring European counterparts had already enforced stay-at-home measures.[11]

These biases—these cognitive distortions—are hardwired in human DNA because they are tied to our most primitive instincts for survival. Human beings are simply not programmed to fully rationalize threat and opportunity, loss and gain. Moreover, our ability to learn from unexpected situations and to absorb and then retain the lessons that crises must teach can be both inefficient and slow.

But knowing this, simply building your awareness of these innate biases, is a critical first step toward overcoming them. Being aware—and prepared—enables us to put into place certain systems, checks and balances, that can help us guard against distorted thinking and sluggish or impaired decision-making precisely when it matters the most: *before* the next crisis strikes.

Breaking the Cycle of Panic and Neglect: The Agency of Your Leadership

Our purpose in writing this book is to give you notice that the next crisis is already heading your way.

We want you to understand that you need to be thinking about that crisis right now, even as the exigencies of everyday life consume much of your time and attention. We want you to think about the things that are stopping you from thinking about the unthinkable. And we want you to take several actions that help you break free from the cycle of panic and neglect. We want to help you to be ready to lead through the next crisis, whatever it is, wherever it comes from, and however it manifests for you and your organization.

You might see this as a tall order. You might ask: Why should I plan for something that may not happen when there is enough in the here and now to occupy my leadership? And you might wonder: How can I even plan for something that I do not yet know or understand?

We intend to show you that planning for the unlikely and the unknowable is not only possible; it is something you can do with relative ease and facility.

We intend to demonstrate that preparing for a crisis is something that you can do every day, in tandem with the regular things you already do as a leader. We aim to show you why an attitude of awareness is imperative and how to build that awareness into your leadership practice. And we will share with you a set of ideas, attitudes, skills, and actions you can adopt and prioritize that will bolster your leadership today and in more "normal" times while immensely enhancing your capacity to lead through a crisis tomorrow.

Even as you read this, another crisis is already brewing.

Perhaps you are managing a crisis right now. Or you have just emerged from a critical situation. Perhaps you are keen to stop and catch your breath in the wake of the pandemic or grappling with the fallout in this new, uncertain, and ambiguous pandemic era. Our message to you, however, is that you should not let your guard down.

In 2020, we learned that because of the complex interconnectedness of things in our globalized world, crises can evolve with unimaginable speed and stealth. What starts in one corner of the planet can spread in days to another and another. And we've seen that we are imperfectly designed to understand and plan for these risks and manage their impact when they materialize. We have seen how easy it is to fall into the cycle of panic and neglect.

But there is another message we want to share with you: You can make a difference. There is enormous power and agency in your leadership before, during, and after the next crisis to reshape events, control outcomes, and build toward a positive outlook for yourself, your organization, and your stakeholders.

If the events of 2020 were frightening and demoralizing, there were still many occurrences and instances of great leadership that give hope and reassurance—people who made decisions that changed the course of the pandemic for organizations and communities.

The "Bubble"

Adam Silver is the commissioner of the National Basketball Association (NBA) in the United States.

In 2020, he made a bold decision—one that made headlines around the world. On March 11, the same day that the WHO declared COVID-19 a pandemic, Silver announced the NBA would be suspending the season for the first time in its almost 80-year history. The suspension would cost the league hundreds of millions of dollars in lost revenue, but Silver was adamant. This was a decision, he told reporters, that was "based on facts."[12]

By this, Silver meant he had looked at the evidence. He had sought the counsel of others—health-care experts and scientists—to make sense of it and determine what it meant for players and for fans. Public health, he affirmed, was of paramount importance, outweighing any other concern. And once he made this position clear, he set about building support and alignment from within the organization. NBA leadership, team owners and players, physicians, trainers, and arena staff were brought on board.

Silver also built a coalition of expertise that extended beyond the boundaries of his organization, tapping into a diversity of skills, prowess, and know-how to manage the situation and devise solutions. The result of all of this? The first and arguably largest "bubble" of the pandemic era—an NBA isolation zone in which players were kept free from infection and played a full 172 games even as the virus raged around the United States and beyond.

Enacting this isolation zone is reported to have cost the league $190 million. But it recouped a stunning $1.5 billion in otherwise lost revenue, without a single case of infection among players or staff during its existence. The NBA bubble passed into organizational protocol as a result of its success—a contingency plan for future crises.[13]

Silver's decision probably saved lives, not just among NBA employees and teams but among its legions of fans around the country. Some have called it a decision that changed the course of the pandemic in the United States in 2020.[14]

It demonstrates the *agency of leadership* in a crisis. The NBA example speaks to the incredible difference that informed, inclusive, and inspirational leadership can make when the chips are down.

In a crisis, your leadership matters. It is the most critical factor that can shape impact, outcomes, and outlook. That's because in a crisis:

- Leaders make decisions that will make a difference in a crisis, for better or for worse.
- Without effective leadership, the impact of any crisis will always be worse.
- The quality of your leadership will determine not only the immediate outcomes of a crisis but also the longer-term outlook once the crisis is over.

A crisis will invariably test your leadership to the very limits of your abilities.

More will be asked of you across every dimension of leadership than in "normal" times. And all of this will happen fast and under uncertainty. In our research, we have outlined the ways in which crises typically make extra demands on the competencies you deploy in normal times. It looks like Table 1.1.[15]

In the next crisis, you will have to

- find a lot of information quickly;
- determine whether it's accurate;
- make sense of that information;
- use it to make decisions, inform your people, and create and enact agile procedures;
- enlist the right resources and talent, to see the way forward; and
- build all of this into your immediate and long-term planning.

Table 1.1. How Leadership Demands Change During a Crisis

Leadership Expectations Under Usual Circumstances	Additional Demands of Crisis Leadership
Articulate a vision and achieve strategic goals	• Maneuver through rapidly changing and challenging circumstances • Draw on others' experience and past crises • See potential opportunities • Take action amid uncertainty
Understand stakeholders and situations	• Broaden understanding of who and what is at stake • Hear diverse voices and understand different groups • Positively influence many stakeholders
Problem-solve and make decisions	• Learn, adapt, and work quickly and ethically • Respond to multiple and differing needs simultaneously • Take bold risks
Manage, motivate, and develop teams	• Create a steadying effect • Inspire crisis leadership capabilities and resilience in others • Galvanize continued commitment
Work across internal and external boundaries	• Coordinate local—and global—needs • Realize implications that cross boundaries • Leverage opportunities to create positive change
Communicate effectively	• Lead in a public manner • Be empathetic, even during times of stress • Develop and express trust quickly
Manage yourself and exhibit leadership competence	• Display commitment toward making a positive difference • Maintain composure • Be resilient

You will have to lead and guide others, reassure them, and provide a steadying influence even amid uncertainty and fear. And you will need to think about the broader ramifications of each action and choice that you make and how your decisions will impact your entire system of stakeholders today and tomorrow.

All of this and more will be asked of you. And you will need to respond under intense pressure—and respond fast.

The one thing you can do to increase your odds of getting it right when the chips are down is to be adequately prepared.

And you need to start doing that now.

Becoming a Prepared Leader

We can't tell you what your next crisis looks like. But we can tell you this: Preparing for the unexpected means expecting it to happen and planning for it continuously. How do you do this?

First, you need to watch for the signs. You need to scan your environment for changes. That will require you to integrate the mindset and the attitude, as well as the organizational processes, mechanisms, and the leadership skills to read your surroundings and do the requisite scenario planning not only to spot the signals but to make sense of them.

Next, you need to have the right processes and systems in place to enable you and your teams to take evasive actions, if possible, to avoid impact. And if impact is unavoidable, you need to ensure you have the time and space you and your people will need to brace for it adequately.

Once the crisis has hit, you need to have the right mix of skills, perspective, and expertise ready and available to help contain or mitigate any damage and limit its spread. You need access to information and knowledge from as many sources as possible to make informed decisions on the go and to ensure those decisions are executed. Communication will need to flow uninterrupted, so you need to have set up your systems and protocols to ensure this happens.

From containing the damage, you need to start to build toward recovery. That means having the information, knowledge, resilience, and creativity in place to set the right goals and objectives, always looking toward the longer term.

Most importantly, you need to be ready and prepared to learn from the crisis. You need to have a learning organizational culture, with processes and protocols in place to surface and share information and to resolve any blockages in knowledge flow. And you need to have procedures in place to capture all the lessons and integrate them into your decisions and planning as you move forward.

Doing these things right will require you to build the teams and relationships forged on trust and openness, and the diversity of skills, knowledge, and perspectives to see the picture as fully as possible. It will also require you to work consciously on your own critical thinking and self-awareness, guarding against bias in your decision-making, deferring to the expertise of others, building the trust to delegate, and enabling collaborative creativity to reframe problems as opportunities wherever possible. It means prioritizing learning from mistakes or failures as they happen. And it means letting go of things that don't work, shifting and adapting as necessary, and empowering your whole organization to collectively rebuild.

Some leaders already do this instinctively. Others will need to make a conscious effort. For all of us, it implies effort and a willingness to put in the work today that will sustain you and your organization to withstand whatever tomorrow holds.

In the chapters to come, we break down how this all works in practice.

People, Planet, Profit . . . and Prepared Leadership

We are living in times of extraordinary change and uncertainty. However, countless risks and crises remain ahead—some foreseeable, others less so. Some we know about; others we do not. As technology, innovation, and our own questing curiosity power quantum advances in our evolution, there are concomitant risks that threaten our well-being and our very existence on this planet—among them the damage occurring to our environment and the climate changes that this will incur. The stakes couldn't be higher.

More than any generation of leaders before us, we have a serious responsibility to be better organizational citizens. We have a serious duty to service core social and environmental as well as financial priorities. Many of us already understand this in the context of a "triple bottom line" paradigm—that beyond the bottom line of *profit*, we have a duty of care to prioritize *people* and *planet* as well (figure 1.1).

But as Prepared Leaders, we also have a duty to prepare our organizations and our people for the worst, to weather the storm and

Figure 1.1. The Triple Bottom Line

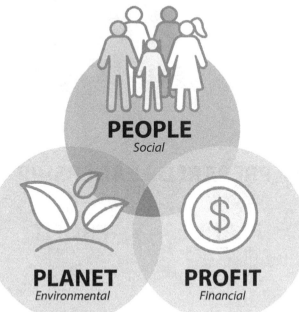

drive positive change in its aftermath. And we believe that this means integrating a fourth bottom line—a fourth *P*—into this leadership paradigm. If we want to survive and thrive in the next crisis, that fourth bottom line needs to be Prepared Leadership, as we show in figure 1.2. And it is as critical to the sustained success of your organization as are people, planet, and profit.

Prepared Leadership will be what determines your ability to deliver in terms of people, planet, and profit when the unthinkable happens. Without it, you will struggle to navigate the chaos, uncertainty, and potential for catastrophe that inevitably accompany crises. Prepared Leadership is what will ultimately determine your success, your viability, your longevity or failure when the next crisis strikes you and your organization.

It took COVID-19 just under two months to overrun our planet. In less than six weeks, it collapsed our economies, emptied our cities and our skies, closed our borders and our schools and colleges, broke our supply chains, and tipped our world into a recession.

Figure 1.2. Prepared Leadership as a Fourth Bottom Line

COVID-19 has left us with great uncertainty about our future. But it has also established absolute clarity about one thing: The unthinkable not only can, but does, happen. And it is likely to happen again.

It's not enough to have a triple bottom line in our desperately uncertain world. You need to make Prepared Leadership your fourth bottom line—and you need to make it an urgent priority for your leadership and your organization today.

Takeaways for Prepared Leaders

- Crises are inevitable, and they always happen.
- Human psychology is hardwired to downplay crises and their impact.
- Leaders must prepare for crises and build that preparedness into their leadership framework.
- Prepared Leadership is your fourth bottom line—it undergirds everything else that you think and do as a leader.

Chapter 2

The Five Phases of Crisis Management

If only we could have seen the clouds that sat like dark
rubble on our own horizon for what they were; if only we
could have worked together to communicate the urgency
of what they would become.
—Helen Macdonald, writer and naturalist

S wifts are migratory birds common to Europe, Africa, and the Middle East. They do something amazing.

Twice a day, these small animals perform what are known as vesper flights. They ascend to the planetary boundary layer—a part of the atmosphere that is characterized by convective currents and air thermals. At this altitude, swifts do more than sleep. They proactively use the wind to assess how weather systems far ahead might change or evolve. They use signs and signals around them to forecast shifts in their environment high above the planet. In other words, the Vesper flight takes swifts to such altitudes that they can read the atmosphere, locate their own position, and plan accordingly.

In an essay published by the *New York Times* in July 2020, British writer Helen Macdonald mused about what swifts can teach us about making decisions in the face of oncoming bad weather. Most of the time, these birds remain below the boundary layer, she writes. But to find out about the important things that will affect their lives, they must "go higher to survey the wider scene, and there communicate with others about the larger forces impinging on their realm."[16]

Not all of us need to make that climb, just as many swifts eschew their vesper flights because they are occupied with eggs and young—but surely some of us are required, by dint of flourishing life and the well-being of us all, to look clearly at the things that are so easily obscured by the everyday. To take time to see the things we need to set our courses toward or against; the things we need to think about to know what we should do next. To trust in careful observation and expertise, in its sharing for the common good . . . [17]

Scanning the environment, seeing the signs, interpreting cues, and making sense of them is something so completely innate in nature, wholly native to migratory animals, and so hardwired in their instinctive behavior and decision-making that it prompts the question: Why do human beings so frequently fail to go higher?

Macdonald's essay highlights something critically important: The best way to survive a crisis is to watch for it and see it coming before it's too late. It is about catching sight of the threat soon enough to avert it or contain the worst and giving yourself and your organization the maneuverability to prepare, mitigate damage, and plan efficiently for recovery.

This is the first phase of crisis management.

As we discussed in Chapter 1, crises will test your leadership to the outer limits of your capabilities. Being prepared, knowing crises will strike, and bracing for them is the one thing you can do to improve your chances of surviving—and thriving—in a disaster.

Most executives are not ready to manage a crisis. That is because most of us do not do what comes naturally to swifts. We do not habitually scan the horizon for changes in the atmosphere that presage trouble. Nor are we systematically alert to signs and signals that something troubling comes our way. Much of the time we are managing the exigencies of what we have right in front of us. Otherwise, we are building plans and setting objectives, strategies, and roadmaps for our teams and organizations that make sense when things are *normal*. Crises catch us off guard time and again. They shouldn't.

COVID-19 caught most of us off guard. But some of us were more prepared than others. History will reveal those leaders who were poised to take evasive measures fast, minimize damage, and prioritize stakeholder well-being, and to emerge from the crisis better off than they were before; and those who fared less well. We'll look at some of those we believe to have emerged better or worse during the pandemic era throughout this book. And we'll explore what they did that shaped their outcomes.

As we said in Chapter 1, some leaders seem to instinctively model the attitudes and skills of Prepared Leadership. Others, less so. For some, Prepared Leadership will feel natural and intuitive. For others, becoming a Prepared Leader will entail something more purposeful and conscious. For us all, bracing for crises and managing them effectively means being a little more like migratory swifts.

This means scanning the horizon for signs of change even before a crisis hits. It means doing this repetitively, developing both attentiveness that pervades your routines and processes and a set of skills, attitudes, behaviors, and cultural norms that will help you make good decisions and respond with agility at each stage or step of crisis management. Because crises unfold across distinct phases.

The Phases

Crises seem to occur instantaneously. But they play out over time. During the last 20 years, as we've researched crises, we've seen five distinguishable phases that characterize crisis management.[18]

When we think about crises, we tend to think about damage control or limitation. In fact, this is only one element. There are things that happen before we get to the point of firefighting, and things that happen afterward: Scanning, preparing, managing, recovering, and reflective learning all form part of the whole.

Your first step toward becoming a Prepared Leader is to grasp that each of these different phases entails specific skills and behaviors to manage proactively, systematically, and effectively. The key thing is to remember that as a Prepared Leader, *you* have agency. You can act at each one of these different phases and make a huge difference in the end result.

Let's break down the five phases of crisis management.

Phase 1: Early Warning and Signal Detection

We know that crises happen. We just don't know where, when, or how they will strike, or what kind of crisis they will be.

Some crises are natural disasters or acts of violence. These crises are harder to foresee, though the signs might still be apparent.

Most crisis situations don't fit into this category, however. Most are preceded by early warning signs—hallmarks you should be able to detect and interpret.

But as we saw in Chapter 1, a raft of human behavioral biases can impair this process. These include feelings of invulnerability—bad stuff happens to other people—as well as a hardwired tendency to focus on the here and now and forget about tomorrow.

History is also full of instances when the poor decision-making or (mis)management of the organization itself contributes to the blind spots that mask an impending disaster. Take one well-known case that predates the pandemic era.

In 2014, senior executives at the German car manufacturer Volkswagen raised concerns about certain engine software and carbon emissions. There was a real risk that US regulators would find compliance issues with its Jetta model. Yet VW leadership chose to ignore these signs and carry on. Martin Winterkorn, the former CEO, dismissed the concerns as "technical issues" due to a few "unexpected" conditions. His leadership backfired in 2015 when the company became embroiled in an emissions cheating crisis that made headlines all over the world and cost it a stunning approximately $30 billion in fines and penalties, as well as the settlement of more than 500 class-action lawsuits. The scandal cost several senior VW executives their jobs—one received a prison sentence of seven years— and ousted Winterkorn from the company's driving seat.[19]

Dieselgate, as the emissions scandal came to be known, could have been a failure to spot the warning signs. It could also have been the result of actual, calculated wrongdoing or fraud on the part of senior decision-makers. But it teaches us the importance of vigilance and the continuous scanning of your environment, your organization, and your culture for cues and signals that you can interpret and understand, because it can ultimately help you avoid crises.

Phase 2: Preparation and Prevention

Once you have detected the signs, the next phase is about enacting proactive measures that can (ideally) prevent the crisis, or at least help you brace for its impact.

When the National Basketball Association's (NBA's) Adam Silver decided to suspend the league's season, it was one of the first high-profile responses to the crisis in the United States. He made the decision amid enormous uncertainty and some time before many governments around the world (including the US government) had enacted restrictions on large gatherings. But his bold decision exemplifies what we mean about reading the signs and acting. The NBA's preventive measure curtailed the risk of contagion among basketball fans and may have helped change the early course of the pandemic in the United States.

Similarly, though some countries were slow to act at the start of the pandemic, others acted quickly. Jacinda Ardern, the prime minister of New Zealand, screened travelers on arrival from China as early as January 2020. And although New Zealand's zero-COVID policy proved an impossible feat to achieve over the course of the pandemic, Ardern's decisive leadership at this phase of the crisis ensured the country had one of the lowest rates of cases, deaths, and civic restrictions at its first peak.[20]

It's important to understand that we cannot prevent all crises. Sometimes, they are unavoidable. But you can prepare by prioritizing preventive or preparative activities, like creating crisis policies and procedures, identifying a crisis response team, and building crisis drills into your operations—because crises can be mitigated and even, at times, turned into positive outcomes.

Phase 3: Damage Containment

When a crisis does strike, what happens next is critical both in terms of containment and damage control. It also determines how you and your organization will progress to the next phase: recovery.

The goal at this stage is to limit financial, reputational, or even existential threats to your organization and stakeholder ecosystem. Depending on how localized the crisis is, one objective may be to contain its encroachment into otherwise unaffected areas of the business or environment.

Containment and damage limitation generally occupy lots of time during a crisis, and this is the phase most people think of when they think about a crisis. It's key to remember that most crises can be contained by limiting the reputational, financial, and other threats to survival.

Although the NBA and others showed decisive and empathic leadership during the pandemic, others emerged with their reputations tarnished. UK pub chain JD Wetherspoon made headlines for the wrong reasons in early 2020 when group chairman Tim Martin announced that his 43,000-strong workforce would not receive any salary during an initial lockdown phase. Instead, he encouraged his staff to look for jobs at the UK supermarket chain Tesco, which was hiring for food distribution at the time. The backlash was as immediate as it was widespread. UK PR firm Hanover described Wetherspoon's approach as "toxic," adding that the organization's reputation gap would be a "chasm that will be hard to close." After all, asked Hanover, "If you have a choice, why would you actively choose to work for Wetherspoon's?"[21]

Phase 4: Recovery

The social network Nextdoor made headlines in the United States in 2015. The hyperlocal platform had launched a few years earlier, connecting households in the same areas and enabling them to share useful information, recommendations, news, and events. But when press reports revealed that users were leveraging the site to racially profile others, reporting "suspicious behavior" on the part of African American and Latino neighbors, Nextdoor's leadership had a full-scale reputational crisis on their hands. They got to work quickly.

A small but diverse taskforce was assembled to unpack data and surface information based on that data. They quickly came up with a solution. Nextdoor's operations team received diversity training; its community guidelines were overhauled and communicated; and its app was redesigned. The result? Within months, Nextdoor had reduced racial profiling on its platform by 75%, according to *Harvard Business Review.*[22]

One of your most ambitious goals in crisis management will be to recover: to recoup time, resources, and revenue lost and to bounce back—or, actually, to bounce forward, better than before.

Business recovery is your North Star. But making it happen takes commitment. It means looking at the crisis in all its dimensions, building the right team to access as much information as possible, and taking decisive actions with transparency. It is also contingent on determining the right short- and long-term goals and initiatives to drive recovery as fully as possible.

Phase 5: Learning and Reflection

As we have seen, the COVID-19 crisis emerged from a cycle of panic and neglect. Neglecting to learn from a crisis will be detrimental to your firm when (not if) the next crisis strikes.

We know organizational learning is the process of acquiring, interpreting, acting on, and disseminating new information across a company. In crisis situations, however, a real risk is that reactive or defensive leadership can create a barrier to learning. It's important to stress that even when you take a learning stance, you are still subject to the previous phases of crisis management.

You should also dig deep into any underlying organizational factors that contributed to the crisis and prioritize necessary changes in firm systems and procedures. Reflecting and finding ways to leverage the crisis experience will lead to the prevention or mitigation of future crises. Investing time in a post-crisis review can often lead to a future state that is even better than the pre-crisis status quo.

Breaking crisis management down into these five phases will help you rationalize what is at stake and what you need to do at each phase.

From here, we can identify the kinds of skills you need to progress from one phase to the next. Effective crisis leadership requires several critical competencies that go beyond day-to-day general management aptitudes.

Simply put, in a crisis, more is expected of your leadership. In our research, we have spent years looking at the stakes and the demands put on leaders, both in normal circumstances and crisis situations, as we shared in Table 1.1 in the previous chapter.[23]

Prepared Leadership is the ability to lead under these amplified pressures and demands. It is the capacity to confront threats and take the right risks, precisely at the moment when our human tendency is to defend, retreat, and avoid threats. During times of crisis, Prepared Leaders need to be able to expand their skill set to meet these new demands and leverage positive change for themselves, others, their organizations, and their communities.

In the next chapter, we look at these skills and how you can deploy them in the different phases of crisis management as a Prepared Leader.

Takeaways for Prepared Leaders

- Crises seem to happen instantaneously, but they play out over time.

- There are five distinct phases in crisis management: seeing the signs, preventing or bracing for impact, containing or limiting damage, driving recovery, and learning from the experience.

- Prepared Leaders have agency across each of these phases.

- Leading in these phases and managing the crisis effectively will make more demands on your leadership than under normal circumstances.

- As a Prepared Leader, you will need to expand your skill set to respond to these demands.

Chapter 3

The Nine Skills of Crisis Management

*We dramatically flattened the communications hierarchy,
using live video to distribute our message effectively and
engage in an open dialogue with our employees. We stayed
on the calls until every question was answered. This helped
ensure everyone was on the same page as decisions
were being made rapidly.*
—Mark Aslett, chief executive officer, Mercury Systems

Mark Aslett knows plenty about crises. As a young man, he worked as an apprentice in the shipyards of Sunderland, a port city in England. His first professional experience happened during a bleak economic downturn, one that saw swaths of workers laid off or going on strike as the local shipbuilding industry collapsed. The impact of this economic crisis on the community, the hardships borne by families struggling to pay their bills, left an indelible mark. It shaped Aslett's values, approach, and *skill set* as a leader. He went on to become CEO of the aerospace and defense electronics company Mercury Systems. In 2020, he took first place in Glassdoor's list of the "25 Highest-Rated CEOs During the COVID-19 Crisis in the US."[24]

Aslett's leadership and the skills that he deployed during the pandemic are worth examining in detail.

When COVID-19 sent the United States into lockdown in March 2020, Mercury Systems had already been monitoring the virus for several months. Aslett set up a crisis response team to track developments, process data, and provide daily updates, which were then communicated to the entire organization in a timely and systematic manner. In the first response team meeting, Aslett worked with colleagues to define three priorities: the health, safety, and livelihoods of employees as an anchor to primary decision-making; mitigating the financial risk to the business; and continuing to deliver on commitments to customers and stakeholders.

One of the first actions Aslett's crisis response team undertook was to flatten communication hierarchy and use live video to share messages and communicate with the workforce. Managers convened daily and then weekly over the course of the crisis. Other actions included suspending employee terminations or layoffs, providing on-site staff a monthly food delivery and childcare credit, doubling overtime pay, resetting paid sick-leave balances, and establishing a $1 million COVID-19 relief fund to support employees and their families.

"When we established the emergency COVID-19 relief fund at Mercury, I did it with Sunderland in mind," he said. He added:

Early in my career, I remember thinking that if I was ever able to positively affect the quality of someone's life through the decisions that I make, then I'm going to try to do that. To me, it's about leading with purpose. Our purpose is innovation that matters, by and for people who matter. We put employees at the center of our purpose statement. This served as an anchor for our COVID response which, in turn, led to record financial results over the last five-plus years.[25]

In 2020, Aslett's business posted one of its best fiscal years on record, despite incurring roughly $2.6 million in pandemic-related costs. According to Aslett, one of Mercury's shareholders told him, "The way in which you should view it is it's another investment in your employees that will generate a multiple of that investment over time. The empathy and caring you guys have shown will be paid back by the loyalty and productivity of employees going forward."[26]

Mercury Systems is an example of an organization that not only survived but thrived under crisis. And we believe that its CEO is a Prepared Leader, a clear example of the leadership skills and aptitudes you will need to model before, during, and in the wake of the next crisis.

In Chapter 2, we looked at the five different phases of crisis management:

- Phase 1: Early warning and signal detection
- Phase 2: Preparation and prevention
- Phase 3: Damage containment
- Phase 4: Recovery
- Phase 5: Learning and reflection

In our many years of research on crises and crisis management, we have identified nine critical skills that Prepared Leaders will need to deploy at each of the five phases of a crisis. These competencies will be familiar to you as a leader, but they take on new dimensions and unique urgency in the context of crisis.[27]

We have grouped these skills in figure 3.1 to show you when you will be called upon to use them most—how these different skills will be urgently required at each of the five phases of your crisis management. Some of these skills will be called into play more than others, at each specific juncture.

These nine skills will help you lead your organization through the next crisis as a Prepared Leader:

1. Sense-making
2. Perspective-taking
3. Influence
4. Organizational agility

Figure 3.1. The Five Phases of a Crisis and Nine Supporting Skills

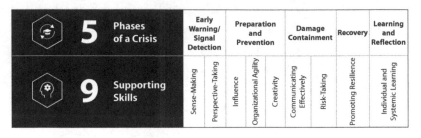

5 Phases of a Crisis	Early Warning/ Signal Detection	Preparation and Prevention	Damage Containment	Recovery	Learning and Reflection
9 Supporting Skills	Sense-Making / Perspective-Taking	Influence / Organizational Agility	Creativity / Communicating Effectively	Risk-Taking	Promoting Resilience / Individual and Systemic Learning

5. Creativity
6. Communicating effectively
7. Risk-taking
8. Promoting resilience
9. Individual and systemic learning

As you are looking for signs of a crisis in Phase 1, you will want to prioritize sense-making and perspective-taking. Then, in the preparation and prevention phase, it becomes important to exert your influence, optimize agility, and deploy creativity.

Getting into the damage-containment stage is where effective communication and risk-taking come to the fore. And as you drive recovery, you will focus on strategies to build organizational resilience.

Finally, in the learning phase, as you emerge from the crisis, your key objective will be promoting an individual and systemic learning orientation so that you fully leverage the lessons from this crisis and prepare for the next one.

You will deploy the nine skills or supporting competencies across the continuum of your crisis management. They are, furthermore, skills that pertain to effective leadership in "normal times." When a crisis hits, however, they become hugely important.

Let's break them down and group them in terms of the five phases of crisis management. As you read through the next part of this chapter, try to reflect on how you model these skills in your day-to-day life, and whether there is work you might want to do in each area as you prepare for the next crisis.[28]

Skill 1: Sense-Making

It's one thing to spot the signs and signals of a looming crisis. It's another to make sense of those signs. To do so, you need to be able to decipher warnings from noise and identify the kinds of imbalances or systemic inequalities that can lead to a crisis. And you need to be able to take a broad set of information from different sources and synthesize it all into meaningful and relevant decisions and actions.

You might think that sense-making is a standard skill for any strategic leader in all circumstances, and you would be right. But when a crisis gathers, sense-making becomes more complex. This is because crises posit a situation or set of circumstances that are new or different, and we often struggle to make sense of the atypical. Remember the cognitive biases we looked at in Chapter 1. It takes Prepared Leadership to push back against our human tendency to downplay or delay.

As a Prepared Leader, you will be able to determine real warning signs and assess the threat without falling into the cognitive traps of ignoring or minimizing risk. How can you do this? Start by asking yourself three simple questions when something looks wrong:

- Are there any circumstances in which these warning signs could develop into a real-world problem, situation, or event for me and my organization?
- If so, what kinds of implications might there be for our stakeholders?
- What are actions my team and I can take about this potential problem, situation, or event right now?

Aslett's team spotted supply chain issues and understood the threat of COVID-19 as early as January 2020.

"That extra couple months helped us move quickly when it hit the U.S. with full force in March," he said.[29]

Skill 2: Perspective-Taking

Perspective-taking becomes even more critical in crisis scenarios. It can make the difference between effective leadership and simple damage control.

If you don't look at the situation from every possible angle, you are more likely to succumb to the types of cognitive distortions and biases that affect the way we understand a threat. You will find it harder to understand all its dimensions. You will be more prone to the *anchoring effect* we looked at in Chapter 1—sticking to one interpretation of a risk even as it evolves or changes. You'll find it more difficult to see how that threat might grow exponentially. And you are in greater danger of overlooking or minimizing something important that could grow or intensify beneath your radar.

Simply put, if you don't have access to as many perspectives as possible, you will fail to see the big picture, and you will be unprepared when a full-blown crisis hits.

To become a Prepared Leader, you should reflect on how you hear and incorporate other viewpoints and perspectives into your sense-making. Ask yourself these three questions:

1. Do you currently have access to diverse voices and sources of information within your team or organization?
2. Do you routinely build other team members' ideas or feedback into your decision-making?
3. What systems or processes might you need to put into place to surface and capture multi-stakeholder perspectives?

In Chapter 1, we looked at the example of National Basketball Association (NBA) commissioner Silver. When he decided to suspend the league's season for the first time in history, he wasn't acting alone.

He had assembled a diverse group of individuals around him, tapping into as many perspectives as possible as the NBA navigated its response to the pandemic. That group wasn't limited to NBA leadership. He communicated regularly with medical experts, among them the former surgeon general under President Barack Obama and a renowned AIDS/HIV research doctor who helped treat Magic Johnson after his HIV diagnosis.

"Silver relied on relationships he had formed to help him understand [the] coronavirus and its potential impact. One of Silver's strengths, beyond his intelligence and marketing skills, is his ability to maintain connections, never knowing when someone might be able to help," *USA Today*'s Jeff Zillgitt wrote.[30]

Skill 3: Having Influence

When the next crisis hits, you will need influence. You will need to ensure that different and multiple stakeholders can follow instructions, make their own decisions, and perform actions that will often sit outside their routine procedures. This is particularly important in the second phase of a crisis: preventing it from happening or bracing for its impact.

Getting other people to act quickly in the face of an oncoming crisis is contingent on communicating your ideas clearly and rationally. You'll have to bring everyone on board and have them trust in you and believe in your leadership. To become a Prepared Leader, you need to be able to align, mobilize, and reassure others, even in tenuous situations. A huge part of having influence in a crisis comes down to your ability to *inspire* others. That ability is tied indelibly to your capacity to make good decisions based on sense-making and perspective-taking—and to do so in a transparent fashion.

We want you to think about your own influence. Be honest about your practices and ask yourself these questions:

1. In your leadership practice, do you prioritize trust and transparency?
2. Do you delegate to those with different expertise or knowledge?

3. Do you communicate your decisions clearly and explain why they matter?

For Silver, having thousands of people align around an idea—the NBA bubble—and take actions counter to experience and intuition meant exercising tremendous influence. Here's what *Forbes* has to say about it. And as you read this, think about the trust, *perspective-taking*, and the coalition of diverse expertise that was put into place to pull this off.

> The NBA bubble is most like a culture change in that, at its core, it was about changing the individual behaviors of thousands of people in pursuit of a common goal—the season being played. It would be easy to dismiss the accomplishments of the NBA bubble by pointing out the relatively small size of the endeavor. But that would ignore the complexities of having to deal with the autonomy of the owners, the egos of the players, the financial interests of the broadcasting partners and the relative freedom of the thousands of Disney employees, most of whom were going home each night and returning the next day.[31]

Skill 4: Organizational Agility

When new and urgent situations arise, you need to be able to empower others to respond and to change course quickly when necessary. And no matter how agile you might be as an individual, driving organizational ability requires you to broaden and integrate your sensemaking, perspective-taking, and influencing skills as a Prepared Leader. This helps ensure your teams and organization adapt to shifting circumstances—to risks as well as opportunities.

In Chapter 1, we talked about crisis management as a simultaneous requirement to lead in the weeds—in the here and now—while leading strategically and thinking about longer-term goals and recovery. At different points in the crisis, particularly when you are trying to prevent it or prepare for impact, you need to step away from managing the immediate to think about the bigger picture. This means having the organizational ability to delegate with certainty.

Here are three questions for you to ponder as a Prepared Leader in terms of your organizational agility:

1. Does your organization respond deftly to change, or do hierarchy and processes create bottlenecks?
2. Do your teams currently have the autonomy to make critical decisions?
3. What practices and procedures can you put in place now that might drive greater autonomy and agility?

Skill 5: Creativity

Creativity is a critical leadership skill in terms of spotting and leveraging opportunity and problem-solving. To become a Prepared Leader, you will need to deploy creativity in the way you recognize organizational vulnerabilities and in how you plan for multiple atypical contingencies. For instance, scenario-planning is a creative process particularly important in the prevention and preparation phase of crisis management. Used effectively, scenario-planning might mean you avert disaster.

Let's go back to the NBA's Silver.

After Silver and his team suspended the season, he gathered information and continued to *make sense of the signs* and integrate *broadened perspectives* into his decision-making. Silver was able to come up with a creative solution by June: to resume the season inside a "bubble." This featured a system of comprehensive health and safety protocols, including distancing, mask wearing, handwashing, and routine testing—that meant everyone, from players to directors, would remain COVID-free across more than 100 games. It also meant that the league crowned a champion that season.

It's also worth remembering that Silver used his *influence* to get buy-in and secured the *organizational agility* to change tack even as the pandemic raged around the United States. It was as creative a decision as it was bold.

Here are three questions concerning your creativity for you to think about as a Prepared Leader:

1. Do you encourage people in your organization to think creatively during a crisis?
2. Are there examples of creative solutions to past crises that worked well for your organization?
3. What practices and procedures can you put in place to encourage more creativity?

Skill 6: Communicating Effectively

All leaders need to be able to always communicate effectively. But in a crisis, Prepared Leaders are called on to do three more things. Ask the following questions:

1. Can you relate to multiple and diverse stakeholders seamlessly and quickly?
2. Do you convey urgency, immediacy, and strength of purpose amid great uncertainty?
3. Can you inspire confidence, provide reassurance, and connect to the emotional needs of many people?

Communicating effectively is a critical skill that plays a major role in every phase of crisis management, but particularly as you work to contain or limit the damage. Getting it right will require empathy, transparency, and trust—influence and perspective-taking—as well as systems and protocols in place to reach as many stakeholders as possible—organizational agility.

As you think about how you communicate in your practice, look at what Mercury System's Aslett has said about it:

Organizationally, one of the biggest things we did was changing how we communicate, given the speed at which the pandemic was moving. We dramatically flattened the communications hierarchy, using live video to distribute our message effectively and engage in an open dialogue with our employees. All people managers attended video calls—daily at first, and then weekly—consisting of 20 to 30 minutes of prepared remarks followed by an open forum. We stayed on the calls until every question was answered. This helped ensure everyone was on the same page as decisions were being made rapidly.[32]

Skill 7: Risk-Taking

Crisis situations are inherently risky. They represent challenges new and atypical. When the next crisis happens, you may have no previous experience or frameworks to help you forge ideas. And that means that as a Prepared Leader you are going to have to take risks at a moment when you will want to take them least.

In a crisis, as we have seen, human instinct can make us want to downplay or minimize a threat we don't truly understand. We also don't want to make mistakes that could make things even worse. But here's the thing: Mistakes are going to be *inevitable*.

To become a Prepared Leader, you need to understand this. And you need to understand that in a crisis you have to act in an urgent and decisive fashion. You need to surface information and perspectives, exercise creativity and influence, and move quickly from prevention or damage limitation to recovery.

Iterative and agile risk-taking are the hallmarks of Prepared Leadership, particularly in the damage-limitation or containment phase of a crisis. Now, as you ask yourself how you take risks in your leadership, think about how risk-taking in a crisis ties to the following:

1. Sense-making
2. Perspective-taking
3. Influence
4. Organizational agility
5. Creativity
6. Communicating effectively

Here's how journalist Dan Wetzel saw it in the context of the NBA case:

> Silver has always been a strong leader for the NBA. He's made mistakes. He's struggled occasionally. His ability to forcefully and convincingly explain his viewpoint though has always been his strong suit. Here was a smart, sensible, serious person making a very big decision that would cost his business incredible amounts of money, and then laying out in clear and concise ways why it had to be done.[33]

As a Prepared Leader, you should ask yourself three questions about risk-taking:

1. In the past, how have you reacted to making mistakes during a crisis?
2. What are some examples of mistakes you or your team have made during a crisis, and how did you respond to them?
3. What practices and procedures can you put in place to learn from mistakes?

Skill 8: Promoting Resilience

In the wake of the COVID-19 crisis, as businesses and communities moved toward recovery, the word *resilience* became prolific in media and literature. People wanted to know how they could make their organizations more resilient to future threats and how to bolster our defenses in the face of new, unknown crises.

In our research, we have found that resilience ties to *people*. The resilience you have in your organization is directly linked to the competence and effectiveness of your workforce.

As a Prepared Leader, you will face challenges on all fronts when the next crisis hits. You will need to put out fires (while keeping your strategic objectives front of mind), protect your revenue stream, and manage your organizational reputation. But you will not be able to do any of this without optimizing and empowering your most valuable asset.

Promoting resilience is about *empowering your people*. It's about giving them the autonomy, opportunity, and support to grow, learn, experiment, make decisions, and pursue courses of action with confidence. Promoting resilience is also about diversity of perspective. It's about building teams with different experience and expertise and ensuring that diverse perspectives are welcomed, valued, and shared proactively.

Here are three questions to think about as a Prepared Leader:

1. Do you actively encourage your people to develop their knowledge and skills, and if so, how? Do they have the space to make and share mistakes?
2. How diverse are your teams in knowledge, experience, and expertise?
3. Is there scope within roles, responsibilities, and activities that speak to stretching and strengthening?

Skill 9: Individual and Systemic Learning

In Chapter 1, we discussed the cycle of panic and neglect.

Leaders and organizations who fail to learn the critical lessons from a crisis—and chief among these, perhaps, is that crises happen again and again—will trap themselves within this cycle of panic and neglect.

The fifth phase of crisis management is about learning from the experience. And in essence, it is the most important. Because no matter how you emerge from one crisis, unless you learn its lessons, you will remain susceptible to similar threats over and over again.

To become a Prepared Leader, you need to pursue learning opportunities in every problem. That means being conscious and proactive about the acquisition of new skills and information and implementing real change as a result. These changes can be individual to people or systemic to your organization. A Prepared Leader will be able to integrate both.

Learning is such a critical skill that it is in many ways the lynchpin of Prepared Leadership. Without learning, you will be vulnerable to future crises. You will be unable to leverage the critical shifts in attitude and skills, process and systems that will bolster your resilience to threats. Without the ability to learn, you will remain unprepared.

In Chapter 9, we return to the critical topic of learning, what stops us from learning, and some of the things that you can do, as a Prepared Leader, to foment a systemic learning orientation across your organization.

For now, ask yourself these questions:

1. How do I learn in real time? How often do I ask myself: What can I learn, and how can I make things better?
2. What mechanisms are there in my organization to capture learning and share it?
3. Is my organization ready and agile enough to enact the lessons and implement change?

So far, we have looked at the hallmarks of Prepared Leadership and why being prepared will empower you and your organization to emerge stronger from a crisis. We've broken crisis management down into its five constituent phases, and we've outlined nine core crisis competencies that you need to deploy to manage across a crisis, and at each phase.

At this point in our journey, you are already in better shape to lead the next crisis. You've understood that crises are inevitable and that you have great agency as a Prepared Leader to shape outcomes and outlook when disaster strikes.

In the next chapter, we dig deep into decision-making: how it works, what can undermine it, and what a Prepared Leader can do to optimize it.

Takeaways for Prepared Leaders

- Crises will put enormous pressure on all your leadership skills.

- There are nine specific skills or competencies that you will need to deploy in a crisis.

- Some of these skills will come to the fore at the different phases of your crisis management.

- Working on these skills now will help you prepare for the next crisis and will also enhance your day-to-day leadership practice.

- Learning is perhaps the most critical skill in Prepared Leadership.

Chapter 4

Making Decisions Under Pressure

A wide range of voices and perspectives make us stronger.
This has proven to be invaluable as we have widened
our circle of influencers and brought more diverse
voices and perspectives to the table for every
tough decision we have made.
—José Cil, chief executive officer,
Restaurant Brands International

When lockdowns and stay-at-home orders were implemented all over the world in 2020, the restaurant industry took a hammering. In the United States alone, estimates put the drop in revenue at 66% at the peak of the pandemic, while job losses totaled more than 2 million.[34]

Amid this news, some leaders made interesting decisions.

On September 3, 2020, even as the pandemic continued its grim work across the globe, Burger King made an announcement that captured the attention of the world's press.

José Cil, the CEO of Burger King's parent company, unveiled a blueprint: a wholly new type of fast-food restaurant, he said, that would set the standard in the post-pandemic era. He called it the "Restaurant of Tomorrow."

What did it look like? To start, Cil and the senior leadership team at Restaurant Brands International (RBI) had leveraged in-house talent—their design team, tech, operations, and food-innovation functions—to reduce the physical footprint of traditional Burger King restaurants by a whopping 60%.[35]

They all but did away with dining spaces, and elevated kitchens suspended above drive-in access points created space for contact pickup cubbies below, as well as curbside delivery spots for customers placing orders via apps. It represented a significantly new vision for the burger chain—and a not insignificant gamble. RBI went on to announce that all of its 12,000 locations around the world would be remodeled between 2020 and 2030, at a cost of $300,000 to $600,000 per restaurant. But remodeled restaurants would see a sales upswing around 20%, Cil has said.

If the Burger King decision was bold, it was also strategically aligned to industry and tech insights suggesting that the pickup trend—already on a tear before the pandemic—was poised to accelerate exponentially. In 2020, that trend grew by 200% in the first two financial quarters. Meanwhile, globally, the food delivery and mobility market more than tripled in value between 2017 and 2021, according to the consulting firm McKinsey. Even if Burger King's gamble pays off, it remains a bold decision nonetheless—all the more so as it was made amid a global crisis and at a time when the industry was experiencing unprecedented losses.[36] The Burger King decision is a great example of *crisis framing*.

Crisis Framing: Threat or Opportunity?

The way we frame a situation, and how we outline its dimensions in our own minds, affects the way we make decisions about what to do in that situation.

When we frame something as a threat, we hunker down and turn our focus inward. Human psychology is such that we accommodate new pressures in our environment by adapting *ourselves* to them in some way. We tend to hide or to conceal and protect our vulnerabilities. In business terms, that instinct might translate into changing organizational structure, implementing new policies and procedures, or taking measures to reduce costs.

If you frame a crisis exclusively as a threat, your decision-making will be internally focused as you bolster defenses around your organizational vulnerabilities. You'll want to batten the hatches and make decisions protective of your organization and people. Your leadership will be more reactive.

On the other hand, opportunities open us up. We tend to base our decision-making more on the external environment and less on our internal feelings of threat or exposure. In business terms, opportunities invite us to move outside our comfort zones, explore new possibilities, disrupt things, and develop new markets.

If you frame a crisis as an opportunity, you are more likely to make decisions that entail risk. You will probably invest time and resources even when there is no absolute guarantee of return. Faced with an opportunity, you are more inclined to prioritize gain over loss and achievement over failure.

For most of us, crises are predominantly threats. We are inclined to frame them as a danger—to ourselves, our people, our organizations, and our stakeholders. But crises are *ambiguous*. They are both threats *and* opportunities. Yet how you navigate a crisis and how you respond to its threats and its opportunities in your decision-making depends very much on the subjective frame you use.

Stop for a moment and ask yourself this: How do you see the world around you?

Think about your past experiences in your personal and professional lives. When something unusual happens, how do you normally feel? Alarmed or intrigued? Despondent or exhilarated? Cautious or curious? Do you react defensively or have you at times tried to push forward to spot and leverage new opportunities as a chance to do things differently?

What about your team? Do you proactively select for team members who bring in opportunity as well as threat perspectives?

In our own research and in examining others' research, we have looked in great depth at the threat–opportunity dichotomy that describes the way that most of us frame a crisis. We find that in crisis management, truly effective leaders—Prepared Leaders—do both.

They simultaneously protect while exploring the possibilities for change and growth that crises entail. And research has also revealed other ways that Prepared Leaders frame crises—four distinct but overlapping frames or approaches that help Prepared Leaders fully assess the dimensions of a crisis situation and empower their decision-making under pressure.[37]

Crisis Framing: Four Positions Prepared Leaders Adopt

Let's look at the four frames, one by one, and think about how they might apply to you and your decision-making. Then we'd like to ask you four simple questions.

1. The Design Frame

If you frame situations through a design lens, you are more likely to see things as *systems*—rational and mechanistic systems that you can break down into constituent pieces and reassemble according to the changing demands of a crisis. The design frame is useful because it helps you continuously adapt your organization's structure. You'll be more adept at working across silos, for instance, and collaborating with diverse stakeholders to solve problems, gain feedback and knowledge, and make rational analyses of actions and outcomes.

2. The Political Frame

If you adopt a political frame in the way you interpret the world, you are more likely to create environments that enable *constructive conflict*. In a crisis, that means you tend to address problems head on. You are critically aware of different people's perspectives or biases, and you are more adept at negotiating and finding compromises even when there are differences of opinion and outlook. You prioritize trust-building, and you are more adept at selling ideas and proposing solutions that balance the interest of diverse stakeholders.

3. The Human Resource Frame

In a crisis, the human resource frame makes you more likely to focus on the effect on your organization's capabilities and its people's performance. As a leader, you will be mindful of how you can effectively deploy the experience, expertise, and skills of your employees to define the problems you face, and collectively solve them. Leaders who use a human resource frame also tend to create an organizational culture where people understand and embrace the idea that *change is inevitable.*

4. The Cultural Frame

If you look at the world through a more cultural frame, you will tend to assert the importance of your organization's identity and its norms, values, behaviors, and ideology. In a crisis, you and your organization will be more likely to cleave to this strong sense of *culture to stabilize the shocks* and impact that crises entail. If this is your dominant frame, you will need to be flexible and adaptable enough to change or redefine parts of your organizational culture, though, as the needs or threats change during a crisis.

Where do you think you fall in terms of these frames? Is there one stance or approach that you favor more than the others, or do you try to integrate all four when facing a major problem or a crisis?

Four Questions for Understanding How You Make Decisions

As you think about this—and about how you see crises as threats, opportunities, or both—we'd like you to ask yourself four simple questions that leading management scholar Robert Quinn has identified. These questions might give you greater insight into your own thinking and the way you make decisions, especially under pressure.[38]

1. Am I results centered?

Ask yourself if you focus on immediate solutions to present problems or if you are open to exploring how problems are opportunities to envision future change.

2. Am I internally directed?

Ask yourself if you feel a strong need to comply with external or social pressures to avoid conflict or if you have confidence in your own values and assumptions to craft a courageous response to a crisis.

3. Am I focused on others?

Ask yourself if you tend to feel and act with empathy for other people's needs and engage in the kinds of participative conversations that build a feeling of shared identity.

4. Am I externally open?

Ask yourself if you really recognize the need for change and if you are willing to improvise, tolerate failure, experiment, seek feedback, and learn as you respond to environmental cues.

You might want to record your answers and come back to them as you progress through this book. Try to be honest and neutral. Building self-awareness of your personal framing mechanisms is another critical step toward becoming a Prepared Leader. It's a critical step toward integrating greater rationality into your decision-making and being more conscious in your efforts to see all of the dimensions of a crisis and the different cognitive tools that you can use to optimize your thinking and your choices.

Doing this work now will help you make better decisions in normal times. And when the next crisis hits, it will empower you to know where and when you need to focus on damage control and prevention—the moments or situations that demand a threat frame. It will empower you to deploy the opportunity frame to explore options and alternatives as they emerge in real time. And it will help you adapt to vicissitudes of the next crisis, lead constructive conflict, embrace change, and stabilize shocks as they affect your organization.

Building this kind of self-awareness will also help you guard against the cognitive distortions and biases that we discussed in Chapter 1.

There, we looked at these biases in the larger context of the cycle of panic and neglect and our innate human tendency to downplay and dismiss crises until it's too late. But cognitive distortions can also threaten your decision-making when you are living the crisis experience. They can put you on the wrong track and make it difficult for you to correct or change direction even as you are putting out the fires and trying to navigate a way forward.

Cognitive biases can undermine rational decision-making at the best of times. And in the crisis situation, it becomes critically important to keep them on your radar as you frame the threats and opportunities and decide on the actions you plan to take during the different phases of crisis management.

Because they are so important, let's look at these biases once again, this time in the context of decision-making under pressure.

Making Decisions Under Pressure: Beating the Biases

First, let's set out what we mean by decision-making.

Historically, broad consensus exists that decision-making is a process. It is a sequence of steps that we take when choosing one course of action over another. Broadly speaking, those steps look like this:

1. **Define the problem.** Look at it in its different dimensions and from different perspectives to get a handle on what you need to address.
2. **Establish desired outcomes.** Figure out what the most important result is, in order to set priorities.

3. **Look at alternative options.** Ask yourself, if plan A fails, what plan B do you need? It's important to limit these alternatives to avoid "analysis paralysis."

4. **Evaluate each option.** Ask yourself, what happens if you choose one option as opposed to another?

5. **Make your decision.** Weigh it all up to determine the best course of action.

From deciding what to eat or wear, to deciding what to say or do, or what strategy to pursue, rational decision-making is a sequence of complex micro-transactions and trade-offs. Doing it well was considered a staple skill for any leader.

But when the chips are down, when you're under the acute pressure that accompanies a crisis, the process of decision-making is suddenly prone to new stress. In a crisis you are going to have to make decisions about something different, atypical, or even totally new to you. The stakes will be incredibly high. There will be a sense of urgency. Time will be in limited supply. And the decisions you make in the heat of the moment could well have huge repercussions for better or for worse, in the short, medium, and even long term.

So, what can you do?

Broaden Your Perspective

As we noted in Chapter 1, the key cognitive biases that affect our judgment include probability neglect, hyperbolic discounting, anchoring effect, exponential growth bias, and sunk cost fallacy.[39]

We saw that probability neglect and hyperbolic discounting relate to our tendency to dismiss or downplay a threat: *It won't happen to me, and even if it does, it won't be that bad.* These biases are particularly problematic for your decision-making in the first two phases of crisis management: seeing the signs and preventing or bracing for impact.

Anchoring effect is the habit of hanging on the first impressions that we have about a problem and sticking to them, even as the threat grows or changes: *This is how I see it, and nothing is going to change my mind.* Anchoring is detrimental to decision-making in the first two phases, but also in the third phase of crisis management: containing or limiting damage.

Exponential growth bias relates to our inability to imagine how a situation might grow or change. Sunk cost is the way we stick to a solution or a course of action even beyond the point that it is useful or relevant: *This is how I'm dealing with it, and I'm sticking to it.* Exponential growth and sunk cost can harm your decision-making across the first three phases of crisis management and on into the fourth: driving recovery.

As you make critical decisions in terms of spotting and making sense of the signs, preparing your organization for impact, limiting the worst of it, and navigating the road to recovery—recovery that will lay the grounds for learning—all these biases have the potential to

- send you down the wrong path of action from the start;
- keep you on that path even as the situation worsens; or
- keep you on that path to the point that you can no longer effectively contain the damage or recover from the crisis.

Alarming as this sounds, there is one simple thing you can do as a Prepared Leader to protect your decision-making from these cognitive distortions at every phase of your crisis leadership. And it's this: You can broaden your perspective.

As a Prepared Leader, you will make better decisions if you can solicit information, input, expertise, experience, wisdom, points of view, different angles, and frames of reference from as many diverse sources as possible and integrate it into your decision-making. The more inputs you have, the less likely you are to dismiss or downplay something simply because you can't see all of its dimensions. The more eyes there are on a problem, the harder it becomes to be anchored to just one solution or approach. The more people you can turn to at each phase of crisis management, the easier it becomes to get a fresh take on your chosen course of action, no matter how much time or resources you have invested to date.

Not only are we prone to cognitive biases in our thinking, framing, and decision-making. We also have a habit of seeking out the opinions, information, and people that *confirm* our own preexisting attitudes and opinions.

It is no accident or coincidence that many of us inhabit what are effectively *echo chambers*. We like to think of ourselves as rational and balanced in our thinking, yet we gravitate to ideas that not only concur with but that also end up shaping our worldview. A clear example of this is the increasingly partisan way that we consume traditional and social media—the gatekeepers to information.[40]

In 2020, the *confirming effect* of the media—its power to entrench biases and keep people anchored to increasingly polarized views and beliefs—was arguably nowhere more in evidence than in the United States.[41] Here we saw fault lines dividing Americans across political, social, and racial dimensions, much of it fanned by media and social platforms. One of the greatest crises of the pandemic era has been the rise of conspiracy theories tied to everything from US elections to 5G, to COVID vaccinations.[42] Among other things, these conspiracy theories are examples of confirmation bias gone into overdrive.

Breaking out of the echo chamber is hard for all of us. But whether it's the media we read, the social media we use and follow, the friends we choose, or the people we gravitate toward in the workplace, as Prepared Leaders, we all have to guard against the tendency to seek out information, feedback, or input that simply confirms a preexisting belief or a bias.

As Prepared Leaders, we must guard against the cognitive traps that impair our decision-making, limit our awareness, and bind our rationality. And we have to reflect on the ways that we frame our challenges and problems, making that extra effort to see the biggest picture possible—the opportunities as well as the threats—when it matters most: when the next crisis happens.

We started this chapter looking at the case of Burger King. We reflected on Cil's decision to announce a Restaurant of Tomorrow even as the industry was being hammered by the pandemic. And we explored how this decision characterizes the ways that leaders can frame crises as threats and opportunities. How Cil's bet on preorder and pickup trends pans out, and whether Burger King and its parent are able to balance costs and revenue in the next decade remains to be seen. But there's something else to say about Cil's bold move in 2020. This was a decision that was not taken *in isolation.*

In fact, Cil went to lengths to explain that decision-making at Restaurant Brands International, Burger King's parent, was undergirded by "a wide range of voices and perspectives" that together made the company "stronger."

Cil explained RBI's decision-making process in an open letter to his organization, on the value of broadening perspective to optimize decision-making in a crisis:

> In early March, just as COVID-19 was beginning to escalate, we decided to postpone our two-day global senior leadership meeting until a later date. We still invited all our senior leaders together on video conference . . . to talk about the single most important agenda item that we felt couldn't wait—the evolution of our . . . company values. . . . The leadership team we have today is an awesome mix of long-term and new leaders; a group of people with vastly different styles and approaches; but also, a group of people who have spent the last few years working very closely together to shape the company into what we are today. The evolution of our values couldn't have come at a better time in our company's history.

He then quoted the first of these values, describing them as values he had relied on to guide the many decisions taken in the previous few weeks, at the peak of the pandemic. That first value is as follows:

> *A wide range of voices and perspectives make us stronger.* This has proven to be invaluable as we have widened our circle of

influencers and brought more diverse voices and perspectives to the table for every tough decision we have made.[43]

Prepared Leaders seek outside input to safeguard decision-making when a crisis strikes. And they seek counsel from as diverse a range of sources as possible.

Prepared Leaders also understand something else about crises: No one person has all the knowledge or complete skill set to manage the complexity and the relentlessness of a crisis.

Part of the nature of crises is that they don't conform to existing structures. And that means that as a Prepared Leader, you must be agile enough to acquire skills and expertise from different places to meet the very unique challenges that surface.

In short, you need to build a team. And you need to make it as diverse as possible.

Takeaways for Prepared Leaders

- Crises are neither inherently threats nor opportunities; they are both.

- How you frame a crisis can help you make decisions and deploy tactics to drive optimal outcomes.

- Rational decision-making in a crisis is threatened by our cognitive biases.

- Prepared Leaders can counter their biases through awareness and, above all, by seeking out diverse input and perspectives.

Chapter 5

Building the Crisis Team

Team leaders like myself can do fancy things in strategy and finance, but when the chips came down, we had to learn to step aside and allow other experts within the organization to step forward. Accomplishing this and allowing influence to flow more dynamically across the organization was a very powerful learning experience.
—Mark Turner, former London director of commissioning, NHS London; Now group director of strategy and planning, Barts Health NHS Trust

The UK's National Health Service (NHS) is a hugely complex, publicly funded institution. It is run by several bodies, including the UK Department of Health and Social Care, as well as groups and trusts that manage areas like budget, policy, and primary care administration. Throughout its history, it has grappled with acute funding and staffing issues—shortages that have threatened at times to compromise the quality of care offered to patients.

Yet, despite the complexities within its own structure, its challenges, and the pressures of the pandemic, NHS teams across the United Kingdom demonstrated a stunning capacity for agility and transformation in 2020. In the case of London's NHS, staff were able to clear patient backlogs and return to 80% pre-COVID operational capacity by October in that year, even as they were in the process of bracing for the second wave of infections.

Mark Turner is group director of strategy and planning with Barts Health NHS Trust, one of the UK's largest trusts. During the pandemic, he worked as London director of commissioning for the London region of NHS England and NHS Improvement, leading multiple teams in London as they responded. Turner attributes the extraordinary resilience that his organization evinced at the height of COVID-19 to one strategic decision: expanding the crisis leadership team and inviting the expertise of a critical but underused resource into all key decision-making—the expertise of physicians working at the front line of the NHS.

In the summer of 2020, Turner and the central leadership team called in all the top doctors at NHS London hospitals and issued them the challenge to "figure out *between you* how to deliver the very best level of care for patients, given the very stretched resources."[44] Pre-COVID, NHS regional systems and hospitals had operated in what Turner calls a "semi-parochial way," focusing on their own, separate goals and objectives, and prone to a fair amount of rivalry. Loosening the hierarchy and breaking down silos was effectively throwing out a long-established rulebook.

But it had immediate and interesting results. Within weeks, clinicians and managers put together a group of "elective hubs" strategically located in different hospitals across the capital. These were specialized centers, isolated from COVID, where high-volume, low-complexity elective operations and procedures could be performed by physicians on patients from all over London, irrespective of their administrative borough or health-care system. Working together in this way—across organizational boundaries and rivalries—meant that NHS London was able to clear its backlog even as hospitals steeled themselves for a second influx of COVID patients.

"Through collaborative teamwork in the pandemic, we uncovered a better way of working that might have taken decades to come to fruition," Turner said.

Concentrating volume in one area dedicated to one procedure or set of procedures instead of having these distributed across a lot of different places, we were able to create a kind of *focus factory* approach, built on agreed protocols, that achieves two things: First, it leveraged our workforce better, with everyone doing the same thing and working the same way; and then second, it created a virtuous circle of higher volume, which led to better quality, greater efficiency and more shared learning outcomes.

Turner also raises a key point about the importance of diversity in crisis management teams: When disaster strikes, Prepared Leaders will need to surface expertise, knowledge, and insight—and defer to that expertise—to find new solutions.

One of the silver linings of the very dark cloud that is COVID has been unlocking the creativity of our brilliant clinicians. Team leaders like myself can do fancy things in strategy and finance, but when the chips came down, we had to learn to step aside and allow other experts within the organization to step forward. And we had to do that very fast. We had to make way for the very expert clinicians in the NHS to lead from the front. Accomplishing this and allowing influence to flow more dynamically across the organization was a very powerful learning experience.

The Power of Teamwork

Teams usually outperform individuals. When you bring together people with complementary skills, people who are committed to a shared purpose or goal and who hold each other mutually accountable, they usually generate more information, stimulate creativity, and expedite decision-making—especially when tasks are complex, ambiguous, or call for innovation.

But in crises, even the most effective of teams can unravel. Crises like the pandemic throw up a plethora of complex and unfamiliar issues that don't conform easily to existing norms or structures. Had the NHS London leadership pursued a business-as-usual approach— had teams of managers and clinicians taken the usual siloed attitude and focused on their own individual needs instead of their collective needs as a whole—it's likely that outcomes for patients in the London area would have been much worse.

As it transpired, Turner and his leadership team took a very different tack. They looked further into their organization for the perspectives, knowledge, experience, skills, and *boots on the ground* to address these new and atypical challenges.

Turner and his leadership team did four things:

1. They composed a new and diverse crisis team—one that sought new input to solve new problems.
2. They established a common sense of purpose.
3. They created the right setting or culture for this team to collaborate, ideate, and share information.
4. And they empowered the team to act with autonomy and speed.

Turner also did something else critical in a crisis: He *deferred to expertise.*

These five things—four steps and one overarching mindset—are what we believe Prepared Leaders should prioritize when building an effective team to manage a crisis. As Turner says of seeking out diverse expertise and empowering collaboration in a crisis:

Traditionally within the NHS, transformation is driven by people like me: managers and decision-makers from corporate or finance backgrounds with expertise in change management. I got into health care via the regulation route. My job is essentially marking the homework of hospitals—organizing interventions where necessary to address financial or quality-based problems. But I have no actual experience of running or delivering health-care services. And with all due respect to team leaders like myself across the country, we have become *health bureaucrats*, to a certain extent.

But what the COVID-19 pandemic taught us is that we didn't need more bureaucrats when a crisis struck. In this crisis, the critical skills—the people we needed to come to the fore—were those on the front line; the people who actually run the services, and who really understand what it takes to deliver those services when time and resources are scarce, and the odds are hugely stacked against you.

Building a Team to Lead in a Crisis: Four Key Steps

Crises are experienced in different ways by different people at different levels of an organization or ecosystem. Senior decision-makers are unlikely to have the same understanding or insights as those who directly interface with customers or those grappling with the operational technicalities of the situation.

For this reason, Prepared Leaders should be open to *all* input and perspectives that can help create a solution and improve outcomes, wherever that input and those perspectives surface within the organizational hierarchy.

What does this mean in practice? We believe that as a Prepared Leader, you need to be ready to do the following:

- Make space for other people to stand up, speak up, and contribute as the situation dictates.
- Let go of your ego and be humble enough to allow others to take the lead as the situation dictates.
- Let these things happen spontaneously and without obstacles as the situation changes.

Building a crisis team is like putting together a puzzle. Each piece should play its role and fit well enough with the others to make a complete picture.

We think of this in terms of four key steps.

Step 1: Compose Your Crisis Team

In a crisis, you want to capture multiple perspectives and expertise to understand the crisis in all of its dimensions, and you want to assemble the different skills and knowledge to build truly creative solutions to new problems. How do you do this as a Prepared Leader?

Be diverse, strategic, and inclusive in your thinking. Source diverse competencies that will help you overcome blind spots, make connections, and join the dots. Look all over your organization for this talent—don't stick to the usual suspects or those who volunteer first. And make it a priority to really listen and to value other people's contributions. For Turner, this meant turning the floor over to the physicians who were on the front line and who also had the clinical expertise, in triage and treating patients, to come up with new solutions.

Step 2: Establish Purpose and Accountability

Your goal here is to align different and diverse people around a shared vision, goal, and actions. You want everyone to be working together to achieve the same ends and to feel mobilized and responsible for their part in that. How do you do this as a Prepared Leader?

Be purposeful, clear, and personally accountable. Set out the team's purpose, and establish goals that you can assess and revise at different points. Make it clear you all share responsibility for achieving your goals.

Again, Turner's focused factory approach was built on a set of protocols that were clearly delineated and shared across the wider team. Executives, physicians, nurses, and others were better aligned and informed about responsibilities, meaning they could share information to better leverage synergies and drive efficiencies.

Step 3: Create the Culture

You're going to want your team to feel empowered to experiment, try new things, bounce back (or forward) when things go wrong, and fully leverage all the learning opportunities along the way. That entails building the trust and sharing processes to keep moving forward. How do you do this as a Prepared Leader?

Be empathic, welcoming, open, and tolerant of failure and complexity. Let your team know you don't have all the answers and that you are open-minded. Encourage your team to forge new connections and to unearth expertise from new or different sources. Inspire everyone to share, exchange, and respect all ideas and input—wherever they come from—without blame or judgment. Model this mindset and lead by example.

When Turner and his leadership team turned the table over to the medical professionals in 2020, one of the tactics they used was to run *hackathons*—agile workshops and ideation sessions where physicians, pharmacists, nurses, and other practitioners brainstormed together with executive staff, experimenting in teams to find answers fast.

Step 4: Empower Your Team to Respond and Adapt

You need to ensure your team is free from as many obstacles as possible and that they have everything they need to pursue their objectives—resources, information, and autonomy—even as the situation changes. How do you do this as a Prepared Leader?

Be agile, transparent, and ready to delegate. Minimize all red tape and bureaucracy, and remain as open and accessible to your team as possible. Be ready to share bad as well as good news so as not to minimize real threats or risks, and encourage your people to share feelings of anxiety or stress. Know, too, when to step away and let others take the lead. Understand when you need to focus on the long-term strategy, leaving the immediacy of the crisis to your team, and when it's time to defer to the expertise of others.

Remember what Turner said at the start of this chapter: What COVID-19 taught him and his executive team was that a crisis of this magnitude and immediacy did not require more bureaucrats. To manage the patient backlog and prepare for a fresh inflow of infections, the NHS leaders chose to step back and make room for those who ran the services. That meant bringing them into the decision-making, giving them the freedom to ideate with agility, and deferring to their expertise in formulating and delivering a solution.

Prepared Leadership: Deferring to Expertise

Decision-makers can often be reliable to entrenched thinking about leadership responsibilities and functions. In our research and many years training executives, we've found that leaders often see themselves as the primary—sometimes the single—solution provider.

It's all too common as a leader to want exclusive ownership of the critical decisions because you feel a strong personal responsibility to your team or organization. The buck always stops with the boss, after all.

The problem with this thinking is that it doesn't help you in a crisis. When you and your organization are facing something different, unfamiliar, and atypical, you need access to skills and knowledge that are also perhaps different or unfamiliar to you and your leadership team. And you may need to look for that knowledge outside of the C-suite, at different echelons of your organizational hierarchy—perhaps even outside your organization altogether.

Turner headed up an administrative leadership team of London's NHS predominantly made up of business and finance experts. Yet when London faced the dual problem of clearing its backlog of delayed operations while bracing for more COVID-19 patients, his team realized they had to work with doctors, consultants, and physicians who had practical and expert knowledge of treating the sick and of doing so under extremes of pressure.

Similarly, when the National Basketball Association's (NBA's) Adam Silver needed a handle on what the pandemic might mean for NBA players, teams, and their vast fan base, he knew he had to look for expertise that went outside of the NBA leadership team—and outside of the NBA itself.

Turner and Silver are two Prepared Leaders who understand the need to accede to other people's expertise when you need exceptional solutions to exceptional problems. Their examples demonstrate a core value of Prepared Leadership.

Deferring to expertise as a Prepared Leader accomplishes three things quickly:

1. It gives you access to information, knowledge, and know-how that can make a critical difference to your decision-making.
2. It gives the other members of your leadership team *permission* to also look for broader cues and inputs that will inform their decision-making.
3. It accelerates the flow of information into and around the team when you all need it most.

But it's important to remember that deferring to expertise isn't just about integrating information from others into your own decision-making. When you find the expertise that may help you and your organization brace for impact and contain damage, you may also need to know when it's time to step back and allow others to showcase that expertise—to step up and take a lead when necessary.

Prepared Leadership and All That Jazz

Prepared Leadership in a crisis can be a little like playing jazz.

If you listen to jazz, you'll know that of all music genres, it's the form most prone to *collaboration*. In jazz ensembles, every player takes a turn to lead with their instrument—be that the saxophone, bass, percussion, or trumpet—or their voice. Leadership rotates as the music dictates, and players often *improvise*, taking cues from each other's performance. For the whole thing to work, each player must listen to what the other musicians are playing at the same time. They must truly hear and understand what the music is saying to them—what it is telling them—to be able to decide what notes or harmonies to play next.

The parallel for Prepared Leaders is clear. In a crisis, you need to be able to step back and allow others to come forward when needs dictate. You need to make space for physicians and clinicians, medical experts and virologists, athletes and team representatives—whoever holds the expertise you need at a given point in the crisis—to step up and illuminate a new way forward as needs dictate.

And when you are dealing with the uncertain or unprecedented, you also need to be able to improvise. You need to be able to react inventively, creatively, and effectively—in sync and in tune with your changing context. You need to be able to do so deftly and without fear. Because fear—of the unknown, of failure—can leave you out of time when things are moving faster than you'd like. Perhaps it's helpful to remember that in jazz, a single note is neither intrinsically right nor wrong. It's the note that comes after it that will determine how coherent the whole piece is. As Miles Davis famously put it: "There are no wrong notes in jazz, just notes in wrong places."

Improvising in a crisis means responding to real-time situations in a way that will inform the next set of decisions or actions. It involves simultaneously creating *and* executing plans, because when you're improvising, there is usually no time to follow a conventional sequence of planning, formulating, or implementing a crisis management strategy. Instead, you and your team must constantly adapt to the situation. You must process information on the go. And you must draw on the intuition and cognitive framing capacity of each member of your team in live time.

Let's be clear about one thing, though.

At the end of the day, the final word will still fall to you as a leader to make the critical decisions that will move you and your organization forward, through the crisis and on toward resolution, repair, and rebuilding. To become a Prepared Leader, you should understand that empowering your team to lead is not the same as abdicating responsibility or delegating critical decision-making to others.

Ultimately, it falls to you to take in information and expertise from a diversity of sources and to use your overarching knowledge and experience to identify the best path forward. Ultimately, you still need to decide what to do. And that means protecting your decision-making, as we saw in Chapter 4, and asking critical questions of yourself and others, even as you take cues and leverage the diversity of expertise available to you and to your team.

For us, leading our organizations through COVID-19 meant being purposeful about all these things. We needed to think about how to bring in enough diversity within our organizations to make sense of this crisis, contain its damage, and to be able to delegate to our team members so that we could focus on recovery and learning—and building our longer-term strategy. This meant sourcing information and proactively inviting new voices into meetings. It meant identifying the right people within our hierarchical structures. Who had real access to our students and our executive clients? Who could share how our learning community was experiencing the pandemic and their needs and concerns? And who could we turn to outside of our organizations to shed light on the bigger picture—the technological dimensions of this crisis, its emotional toll, and what it might mean for evolving trends in learning?

It also meant bringing different, sometimes siloed teams together across disciplines, faculty, departments, and administrative groups—reaching into our student and alumni bodies when necessary—and finding tactics to facilitate dialogue. And it meant modeling the transparency, authenticity, and accountability to build trust.

And for us, new to our roles, it meant doing all of this with new teams, new communities of learners and alumni, and new organizational structures and cultures while building relationships in a new organization.

Walking in Mid-Movie

In an ideal situation, before the next crisis strikes, you will have already started to put together and optimized your core crisis team.

Earlier in this chapter, we outlined four steps and a mindset you can use to create your own checklist and identify those areas that you might want to focus on preparing now. Look at your existing teams and structures and ask yourself these key questions:

- Where will I find the diversity of skills, perspectives, and expertise—around my organization and beyond—that I will need to access when a crisis strikes?
- How will I establish purpose, accountability, and clarity around roles and responsibilities when time is short?
- What are the strategies that will help me establish a culture of empathy, inclusion, and tolerance—of failure, complexity, and anxiety and emotional stress—to drive resilience, innovation, risk-taking, and learning?
- Is my leadership open enough to bring expertise in wherever it surfaces, to improvise where necessary—and do I model these values as a team leader?

Prioritizing these questions with your existing team and structures today will mean you are all in better shape to grapple with the crisis of tomorrow.

But crises are unpredictable. We don't know with absolute certainty when, where, or how they will strike, or where we will be when they happen. Crises can happen anytime, when we are completely new in a role, say, or transitioning into a totally different position.

We found ourselves as leaders, grappling with a crisis even as we were finding our feet with new teams, new structures, and new organizations. And walking in mid-movie, inheriting a crisis team, just as a crisis is unfolding all around you, can be a massive challenge even for the most Prepared Leader—as we shall see in Chapter 6.

Takeaways for Prepared Leaders

- Your crisis team should have a clear and common sense of purpose.

- You need to set a culture of collaboration, ideation, and sharing of information across your team.

- Your team should also feel empowered to act and react with autonomy.

- Prioritize diversity, inclusion, tolerance of failure, and complexity.

- Defer to expertise wherever it comes from within your team, outside of your team, throughout your organization, and beyond it.

- Ensure that you and your team have what you need to collaborate, to step back and step up when necessary, and to improvise as the situation changes.

Chapter 6

Inheriting a Team
in the Middle of Crisis

It's having the courage to say to a new team: you know
what, yes I am new, and no I don't have all the answers.
But this is a journey and it's one that we share.
—Wonya Lucas, CEO and president, Crown Media Family

In July 2020, Wonya Lucas became CEO and president of the Crown Media Family Networks, which operates the Hallmark networks. She had to grapple with two challenges.

First, she had to inspire, align, and mobilize an executive team of people she didn't yet know. As their new leader, it fell to her to bring these new colleagues on board and in support of her vision to execute the mission and accelerate the growth of one of the most iconic media companies in the United States. And she had to do this while also navigating all the mutability of a pandemic.

Lucas had held a range of senior leadership roles at well-known media players, including TNT, the Discovery Channel, and Public Broadcasting Atlanta. Yet despite her wealth of experience, taking the helm at a new organization in the middle of a global health crisis was "uncharted territory."[45]

For Lucas, transitioning into new organizations had traditionally been about face-to-face contact. She looked to establish points of connectivity and *humanize* herself as a leader so that her team members could relate to her as a person beyond the job title. But stepping into her role at Hallmark mid-pandemic meant she had to meet close colleagues for the first time via Zoom—an unusual situation and one fraught with the risk of missing the subtle cues and signs that drive human understanding.

Lucas made a decision. Instead of asking the "usual" questions around job roles and responsibilities or the kinds of problems and goals the team was facing, she chose to find out about people's individual hopes and aspirations for the organization. She did this for two reasons. First, she cast her relationship with her new team and the crisis in a positive light. Second, it helped her break down barriers.

Asking people about goals or aspirations for their firms helps create what Lucas calls a "sense of discovery" for people because they get to share their thoughts and ideas, regardless of where they sit within the team structure.

Within her first weeks of tenure, she had scheduled more than 30 Zoom calls with key team members and employees. She told us:

> As a team leader, it's vital to discover who your people are and what motivates them. And in a crisis, this is more important than ever. But it's key to be clear about your objectives. For me this first period was less about sharing my vision or strategy and much more about getting to that human connection and tackling the very understandable perceptions of me as an outsider, as someone new. I wanted to convey a very important message: that I was accessible and that I was there for my team during this incredibly difficult time.
>
> Of course, as a new CEO, you do want to understand what's working and what's not working. But I wanted to learn this within the context of personal, individual motivation. So, these calls were about identifying what my new team saw as their own missed opportunities—things they wished they'd done but hadn't gotten a chance to try. I learned amazing things about people in the process: a passion for cave diving, one team member who kept a pet sheep in Brooklyn—fun, human things that we can talk about when we see each other.

The other objective of these personal calls was to address anxiety; to counter whatever fears my team had about what they might stand to lose with a new and unknown leader, and how things might pan out for them and for the company during a pandemic. To do this effectively meant first *establishing trust.*

Taking up the reins somewhere new amid a crisis, whether inside your current organization or in a new company, you may not have the luxury of walking the halls with your key new people. Lucas walked into crisis leadership *mid-movie* during the COVID-19 pandemic. We had the same experience, taking over the leadership of Simmons and Wharton in 2020. As any leader who took on a new role in a new organization in the pandemic will attest, this meant working intensively, intimately, and over long and sustained periods of time with people we didn't yet know well. And we had to do so under extraordinary pressure and uncertainty, without yet having a clear sense of the evolving situation.

Trust is a huge priority in these circumstances. And as a Prepared Leader, it falls to you to be the primary agent in building bidirectional trust. *You* need to model the way forward. As you make sense of the power, the politics, the strengths, and the values of your new team, not only must you determine whom *you* can trust, but you must also build your team's trust in *your leadership.* For Lucas, accelerating the trust-building process with a new team meant modeling personal transparency and candor. We agree wholeheartedly with her thoughts:

At my first town hall meeting with the wider team I made it a priority to share personal information about myself: my background, my leadership style, and my connection to the brand and its culture. Just as important in times of crisis, I think, is having the courage to say to a new team: "You know what, yes, I am new, and no, I don't have all the answers. But this is a journey and it's one that we share."

Going in as a new leader it falls to you to set the tone, and for me this is really all about accessibility and open communication built on trust. In every meeting at the height of the pandemic, I worked hard to empower my team so that people feel they could communicate openly with me. I wanted them to be able to share personal information with me. And, without always focusing on the negatives, I did want them to feel brave enough to tell me when things weren't working. I wanted them to feel that they had a voice and that they were being heard.

In one of our first meetings, one department told me about a procedure that had been in place since the 1990s—an inefficient practice that ate up time and resources without delivering results. I killed it on the spot. Making that decision—a decision that drew on my own experience as a leader, but one that was directly informed by feedback from my new team—news got around the organization fast. The upward flow of information had led to actions being taken—follow-through where it needed to happen. As a result, people felt heard and valued. We had established trust, and we'd established it quickly.

The Three C's of Trust

In the mid-crisis scenario, trust-building has to happen fast. There is a multidirectional need to rapidly assess each other's integrity, dependability, and ability to do what needs to be done. Psychologists often refer to these things as the Three C's of Trust.[46] They are *communication*, *contract*, and *competence*.

This is how we define these three C's, and how we'd like you to think about them:

- **Communication:** Is there transparency and integrity in the way you communicate with other people and the way your team members communicate with you and with each other? Is communication something you prioritize, especially when you take over leadership of a new team?

- **Contract:** Is there a strong sense of contractual obligation or commitment between you and your team or teams? Do you take care to follow through on what you pledge to do—and do you ensure that your team members do the same?
- **Competence:** Are you confident that you have the knowledge and the aptitudes needed to get critical things done? What about your team members? Do they have the right skill set to execute what needs to be done, and done fast?

It's worth thinking very deeply about these three C's in the crisis setting. Communication is not just about communicating the positives. Crises posit real threats, and it is incumbent on you as a Prepared Leader to tell the truth and face the facts. Downplaying risks is a human behavioral trait, as we've seen in earlier chapters, but it will not help you set realistic goals or build long-term confidence in your leadership.

Conveying the truth and facing the facts—telling it like it is—will establish trust more effectively, however unpalatable that feels to you and your team. To get through the challenges of the crisis, you will need to keep the lines of frank, honest communication open and bidirectional, allowing for doubts, questions, and anxieties as well as the insights and expertise that you will need to inform your decision-making and action plan. Following through on each action of your plan—and requiring that your direct team leads and their key members to do the same—speaks to the contractual commitment and the competence you need to lead through the crisis.

When the National Basketball Association's (NBA's) Silver announced he was going to suspend the NBA season for the first time in its history, he meant it. When Turner and his team turned strategic problem-solving over to National Health Service (NHS) clinicians in London, they saw to it that elective operation hubs had the backing and resources to spring up all over the capital to clear the backlog ahead of the second wave of COVID-19 infections. Lucas not only made it a priority to follow through on every

Figure 6.1. The Trust Assessment Wheel

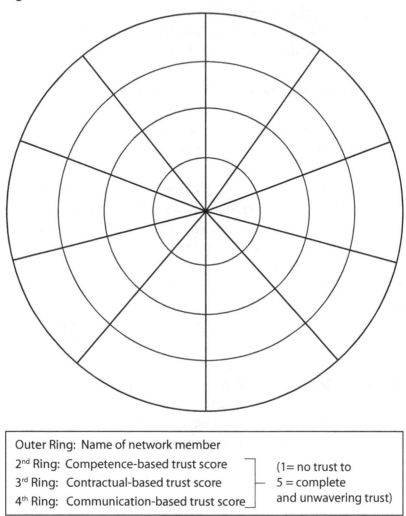

Outer Ring: Name of network member
2nd Ring: Competence-based trust score   (1= no trust to
3rd Ring: Contractual-based trust score   5 = complete
4th Ring: Communication-based trust score   and unwavering trust)

personal decision or promise—she demanded it of her team members too. Prepared Leaders build trust by talking the talk *and* walking the walk.

Erika has developed an easy-to-use tool that can help you reflect on the three C's of trust as you navigate a crisis with a new team or new team members. The Trust Assessment Wheel (figures 6.1 and 6.2)

Figure 6.2. The Trust Assessment Wheel in Motion

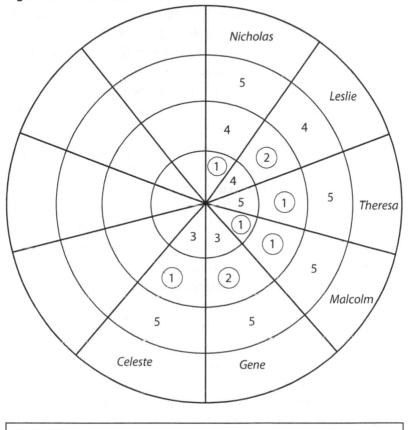

Outer Ring: List names of network member
2nd Ring: Record competence-based trust score ⎤ (1= no trust to
3rd Ring: Record contractual-based trust score ⎬ 5 = complete and
4th Ring: Record communication-based trust score⎦ unwavering trust)

is a simple three-step exercise that you can use to quickly assess the trustworthiness of your key people, and to sense-check the validity of your assessments.[47]

To assess trust in your team, use the segments in the outermost ring to identify key members whose trustworthiness you want to evaluate. Then, for each person (slice of the Trust Wheel pie, so to speak), assign a score from 1 (no trust) to 5 (unwavering trust) for each of the three trust dimensions (competence, contract, and communication). Once you have completed the chart for each member of your team, you have two ways to interpret the assessment. First, by examining the values associated each of the trust dimensions for a particular person, you can discern which type of trust is more or less evident in your interactions with that person. In the sample chart, you will notice that Nicholas was evaluated low for communication-based trust but high in competence. This more nuanced understanding of trust in individual team members provides targeted insight for feedback and performance-management purposes.

In addition to helping you learn more about the trustworthiness of your team, this tool also provides information about your own proclivities for trustworthiness. By examining each ring within the Trust Assessment Wheel, you can see in the example that the evaluator may have a tendency to assume most people on the team are highly competent (mostly 4s and 5s for competence-based trust). Conversely, most team members were given low scores (1s and 2s) for contractual-based trust. While these values may, in fact, reflect the overall team trustworthiness, it is often the case that a preponderance of high or low scores for any particular dimension of trust is more revealing of your own preferences or tendencies to trust or not trust along that dimension.

In "normal" times, the three C's of trust are key. In crisis situations they are critical. Because in a crisis you need to establish *swift trust*.

Establishing Swift Trust

By its nature, a crisis team is usually temporary: an interim group put together to respond to the special and specific exigencies of a crisis.

As such, your crisis team must grapple with a *paradox*: Working together effectively and under pressure requires you to establish trust. But if your team is interim or temporary, assembled hastily and composed of members who may not know you or one another, it's unlikely you'll have had the chance to establish that trust—over time, through day-to-day interactions and fulfilled transactions. In 2020, this was the situation that we found ourselves in when we inherited teams of people we didn't know and who didn't know us, but with whom we were about to go with into battle.

As a Prepared Leader, when time is against you, it's imperative to build what organizational scholar Deb Meyerson terms "swift trust." It is a presumptive and circumstantial trust that pulls your temporal task force together, binding everyone temporarily around a shared sense of purpose.[48]

The good news is that the mechanisms of building swift trust adapt very well to the intellectual and emotional demands that crises make on human beings. Establishing trust fast—taking a psychological and emotional *leap of faith* to collaborate with people you may not know well under stressful and challenging circumstances—is more straightforward in a crisis than in "normal times."

And there are three reasons for this:

1. **Trust requires vulnerability.** In trusting someone, you inherently make yourself vulnerable to that person. Psychology and organizational science tell us that collective or shared vulnerability is a core component of trust. Without it, trust cannot exist. Crises also invariably invoke feelings of vulnerability. In a crisis, people, organizations, communities, and ecosystems are all vulnerable to risk or danger in some way. Put simply, in a crisis, we feel a shared vulnerability that makes it more likely—and easier—to trust other people, even relative strangers.

2. **Crises are inherently ambiguous and uncertain situations.** In a crisis, we focus our time, energy, and resources on trying to figure out how things might evolve, the possible scope of the damage, and those likely affected. In a crisis, we usually don't have the time, energy, or resources to spend second-guessing other people's trustworthiness. We are far too busy figuring out how to deal with problems at hand.

3. **Crises are inherently risky, and so too is trust.** When we trust someone, we risk making ourselves vulnerable to them—

we take that risk. In a crisis, because we're exposed to more risk, we're likely to be more prone than usual to risk-taking to mitigate the threat. Part of the risk-taking we do in a crisis is inevitably linked to trusting others to play their part, to take responsibility, and to follow through as part of the team effort. Put another way, crises tend to force our hand in terms of taking risks—including the risk to trust people we may not know well—because we're all in something together.

But even if crises lend themselves well to establishing swift trust, there are still things that you can and should do as a Prepared Leader to ensure that you and your crisis team have real confidence in each other, in your collaboration, and in your ability to resolve the challenges you face.

Coming into a new organization mid-crisis means inheriting a new team. But it also means inheriting a set of circumstances and several exigencies posited by the crisis that are specific to your new organization and team. For us, coming into Simmons and Wharton mid-pandemic meant learning about the different skills and expertise within existing teams and *how these skills aligned to the demands of the crisis*. Where necessary, we had to be ready to make changes throughout our organizations. We had to be prepared to look outside of our teams to source the capabilities that we needed to manage the pandemic more effectively.

Making changes to an inherited crisis team can be problematic. Even if you don't have members exit the team, you may still have to encourage them to recalibrate the work they do or the way they work. Remember that in a crisis, your team needs to be able to defer to expertise and embrace improvisation, as we saw in Chapter 5.

Part of this may mean bridging silos in your new organization to bring in new perspectives and access to new information. And this may be new to the teams and the people that you lead.

Crises, as we said earlier, can facilitate trust building under exceptional circumstances. They can also posit a need for temporal or interim teams or structures—a focused crisis team or task force—to enact highly targeted responses to the specifics of the challenges you face. Coming into an organization as a new leader mid-crisis can also work in your favor here. Expectations around change may be more generalized by the very fact of your *newness*, and resistance to recalibration or different ways of doing things can be attenuated by open and transparent communication. But you may still face hesitancy.

For us, taking over new teams at Simmons and Wharton meant instituting meetings—lots of them. Like Lucas, we made it a priority to learn about the people we were tasked to lead, understanding their motivations, anxieties, and concerns as well as their diverse skills and expertise. It also meant creating cross-functional meetings to bring in different areas of organizational knowledge and information.

At Wharton, Erika charged team leaders with identifying the one or two team players they relied on most and asking them to attend crisis management meetings. Where individuals felt out of their comfort zone or were hesitant to contribute, this meant proactively inviting them to speak and drawing them out saliently—such was the importance of capturing invaluable insight from people with boots on the ground.

For Lynn at Simmons, structuring meetings with great care was critical. Being intentional about the design of each meeting agenda, pre-agreeing what would be discussed, preparing in advance, and making the fullest use of virtual technology—whiteboards, chat functions, and breakout rooms—was an effective way of engaging the first and second layers of leadership and knowledge that were so critical to understanding the team, the organization, and the best way to respond to the crisis.

Leading any team through a crisis is always hard. In our experience, leading through a crisis when you're new to the role or the organization is even harder. Processing information from new and diverse sources as you simultaneously manage yourself and others can test the most seasoned leader.

Fortunately, there are several tactics Prepared Leaders can put into place that will help surface and make sense of data and input while avoiding information overload.

How to Have High-Performance Meetings

Having a structured approach to the goals and agenda of each meeting with your crisis team will help you focus on the important things. If you are leading a complex organization, your team is likely to be big and representative because you will want to capture as many perspectives as possible and ensure that information is flowing as freely as possible.

A good tactic is to ensure each member of your team is clear about learning objectives ahead of the meeting. As Lynn suggests, you might also want to make good use of *Liberating Structures* for presentations, discussions, brainstorming sessions—simple rules and frameworks that are simultaneously inclusive and result-focused and designed for relational coordination and trust-building.[49] And as Erika practices, you may want to deploy the three dimensions of trust—the three C's—as a rock-solid basis to assess your team's performance.

Leading our teams during the COVID-19 pandemic, we routinely had more than 35 people on video calls, several times a week. We made something explicit early: We did not expect every member to contribute to every meeting. The goal for us was to create a bidirectional platform for shared expertise. In a crisis, you never know where or when that one piece of key information will surface, so it's critical to have everyone in the room. And a diverse team has the additional benefit of ensuring important information can cascade down through the organization, informing everyone's decisions and work.

At the start of a crisis, you will want to have frequent team meetings. They might happen every day, a few times a week, or more ad hoc. And you should be prepared for frequency changes as circumstances dictate. But as a Prepared Leader, it's critical that you know when to extract yourself from crisis meetings to focus on other things.

Remember, crisis leadership is about dealing with the immediacy of the threats at hand while also building the organizational resilience and adapting your strategy to ensure longer-term business continuity. For this reason, Prepared Leaders ensure their teams have a rock-solid understanding of the guiding principles and priorities to do their work, even when you step away. As a Prepared Leader, you need to be able to delegate to your team and empower them to advance the work.

It is critical you communicate the goals, objectives, and reasoning that informs every one of your decisions. Think of this as your North Star. When you are ready to make the transition from being in the weeds to leading your organization's long-term strategy, be vocal with your team about the need to shift your priorities.

For Erika, stepping away from the immediacy of crisis management in 2020 meant two things. First, it was a demonstration of trust—bidirectional trust—between her leadership and her team. Stepping away meant showcasing confidence in the team's ability to carry on the direct management of and response to the crisis without her direct oversight. Second, shifting her focus to more strategic leadership was an opportunity to consolidate all the learning and understanding gleaned during this period. This eventually became "The Wharton Way," a document that highlighted the rich history of the School as well as the opportunities ahead to shape the future of business education. The Wharton Way became the organization's North Star and continues to guide the School's strategy.

For Lynn, accelerating communication, contract, and competency-based trust to empower her team to lead through the crisis meant building greater understanding of what was going on in the broader context—the ecosystem of higher education. One way of doing this was to bring in (and defer to) expertise from outside of Simmons: guest speakers from external organizations, such as Professor David Feldman to discuss the changing business model of higher education and Professor Tyrone Freeman to present on inclusive and innovative philanthropy (or philanthropic) practices.[50]

For both of us, as leaders in education and stepping into new roles, mid-crisis, within long-established, prestigious institutions, meant prioritizing learning: our own learning and that of our teams. We come back to this in greater depth in Chapter 9.

As you lead your new team in a crisis, remind yourself and your colleagues of your overarching goals and what you are collectively trying to accomplish. Be clear that every decision you take together should be anchored by your efforts to protect the most vulnerable. Be sure to share this with your team regularly, whether that team is new, temporary, or long established and accustomed to working together and with you. Build a vision around which everyone can rally. And use this as a springboard for collaboration, empowerment, collective leadership, positive improvisation, resilience, and decisive action.

Leading any team in a crisis will test you of course, whether you are inheriting that team and coming in new amid a crisis or whether you are mid-tenure when a crisis strikes. And as you emerge from one crisis, you need also to be mindful of how you will continue to empower your team and your organization to evolve and to build the skills, the collaborative processes, and the agility to step up and manage the next crisis—wherever that crisis emerges and whatever form it takes. Because, as we have seen, *crises always happen.* Just as one crisis starts winding down, another may already be on the horizon.

The next crisis you and your team face might already be something foreseeable, or it might be less than predictable. It might be sudden, or it might be a smoldering crisis. It might be focused and localized, or it might be something that engulfs the entirety of your organization, your customer base, your community, and your stakeholder ecosystem. And in our interconnected, interdependent modern world, where business, trade, capital, and human beings flow freely from region to region and country to country, the latter is always possible—if not probable. Where a crisis affects one part, the whole can quickly follow.

In our globalized modern world, as COVID-19 all too readily demonstrates, crises can easily become global.

Takeaways for Prepared Leaders

- Inheriting a new team in the middle of a crisis, you need to establish swift and bidirectional trust.

- You can assess these dimensions using the Trust Assessment Wheel.

- In a crisis, you may need to make changes to the team you inherit, depending on the challenges you face.

- You will also need to build bidirectional trust with your new team to be able to step away and refocus your attention on strategic leadership.

- Open communication, contract (following through and following up), and competence remain key—especially if you bring in expertise from elsewhere or outside the organization.

Chapter 7

Managing a Globalized Crisis

All crises are global.
—Marion K. Pinsdorf, author

COVID-19 was the most significant "global event" of 2020, to borrow economist Branko Milanovic's striking description.[51] But it wasn't the only globalized crisis that characterizes what we might now call the "pandemic era."

Social justice, racial tensions, political partisanship in the United States and Europe, populism, poverty and inequality, the intensification of the climate crisis, wildfires in the Arctic, and snow in Texas—the year 2020 saw numerous, oftentimes interconnected crises that crossed boundaries and borders.

For businesses and leaders already navigating the vagaries of the pandemic, 2020 came with a panoply of adjacent globalized risks to monitor, manage, and contain. Some were successful, others less so. Take banking behemoth HSBC.

Relations between China and the United States hit perhaps a new low in 2020, fueled by American anger over Beijing's lack of transparency on COVID-19, perceived political authoritarianism in Beijing, and an increasing trade rivalry between the two superpowers.[52]

HSBC found itself caught in the crossfire of US–Sino animus on June 3 when its CEO, Peter Wong, was publicly photographed signing a petition to back China's controversial new security laws for Hong Kong.[53]

Wong's decision was almost certainly prompted by pressure from Chinese state media for the bank to make its position clear. Nonetheless, this single act undid more than a century of studied neutrality on the part of the bank, which has headquarters in Hong Kong and in the United Kingdom. It cast doubt on its claim to be "apolitical." Worse still, it prompted an immediate and significant backlash across both its internal workforce and its significant shareholder and customer bases in the United States, the United Kingdom, and elsewhere.

Around half of HSBC's shareholders are Western. These include major institutional players such as Blackrock and Norway's sovereign wealth fund. Many of these shareholders have a publicly stated commitment to environmental, social, and governance (ESG) criteria for their investments, which puts them into direct conflict with China's overseas policies.

Wong's dilemma is relatable in some ways. HSBC has invested billions of dollars in China to grow its market share in the world's second-largest economy. Over time it had been increasingly difficult to maintain the balancing act, especially in the face of continuing criticism from both pro- and anti-Beijing camps. For Wong, toeing the line of neutrality had perhaps become all but impossible.

It's much harder, however, to make sense of the decisions and actions that saw another multinational company engulfed by a globalized crisis in the same year.

CrossFit is a multibillion-dollar US fitness brand, once dubbed "most innovative company" by *Fast Company*. But its founder and CEO, Greg Glassman, found himself on the wrong side of public opinion when he became entangled in the furious global backlash over the murder of George Floyd in May 2020.

Floyd's slaying at the hands of a white Minneapolis police officer cast a spotlight on the deep social fissures and systemic racial inequity in the United States. It caused international outcry and mass protests in the United States that quickly spread to other regions, with demonstrators in Europe, Latin America, Africa, and the Middle East signaling their solidarity with the Black Lives Matter social justice movement. Corporate America, too, came out in unprecedented support, with mega players like PepsiCo, Apple, Citibank, Facebook, and Procter & Gamble publicly committing to a raft of measures to combat institutional racism. The US's 50 biggest public companies and their foundations collectively committed at least $49.5 billion to addressing racial inequality—an amount that was unequaled in sheer scale.[54]

Yet amid this, and even as the pandemic continued to rage around the globe, Glassman posted a comment on social media that made light of COVID-19 and the Floyd murder. Responding to a description of racism as a "public health issue," Glassman tweeted: "It's Floyd-19." This, and a slew of remarks leaked to the press, questioning the validity of "mourning" Floyd's death, sparked an immediate public backlash.

In less than a month, CrossFit lost thousands of affiliated gyms across the United States. It lost the loyalty of its customers, and it lost a lucrative sponsorship deal with Reebok. By the end of June 2020, Glassman had lost his job and his company.

He had failed to understand the globalized dimensions of the crisis that he had waded into—and how his words and actions, played out on a public stage, would be construed and interpreted by different groups and stakeholders within his organizational ecosystem and his broader customer bases.[55]

Navigating the Globalized Crisis

When a crisis is globalized—when it simultaneously affects different geographies and markets, different parts of your business, or different stakeholders within your organizational ecosystem—the pressures on you as a Prepared Leader will multiply exponentially.

You will need to be everywhere at once: hands on with what's happening with your immediate team and headquarters while also keeping pace with what's going on across the outer reaches of your organization.

As you progress through the different phases of crisis management—spotting the signs, risks, and opportunities; containing damage; driving through to recovery and beyond—you will also need to do the following in a globalized crisis:

- Understand how the crisis might have an impact across all your *different operational contexts*—people, processes, systems and equipment, and capabilities—internally and externally, in domestic markets and overseas.
- See how things might develop *in different cultural contexts*—across your different markets and stakeholder groups.
- Spot the critical opportunities and the threats that exist for you and your organization both locally *and* globally.
- Identify and deploy the *differentiated resources, tactics, or strategies* you need to avert, brace for, or contain any damage—wherever, however, and whenever necessary.

If yours is a large or complex organization, this can be even more difficult. Parts of your operations or stakeholder segments may be far removed (geographically or culturally) from your centralized point of command. You may also have to manage conflicts of interest or perspective that can intensify quickly. In a globalized crisis, there is greater risk of losing control of events and of those events snowballing, as a couple of high-profile organizations found to their detriment during the pandemic era.

Managing so many moving parts, seeing how things might evolve in different places, in different parts of your organization, and in different cultural contexts all requires you to *manage multiple realities* at once.

It requires you to create a crisis team that is diverse in perspective and expertise and that draws on the insights and the knowledge of individuals from different areas of your organization and external stakeholder community.

It requires you to establish the systems and processes that enable information to surface and to flow freely across your hierarchy and across geographic boundaries.

It requires you to institute an organizational culture that defers to expertise and that invites expertise in—permitting different people to step up and enact leadership in different contexts whenever necessary.

And it requires you to prioritize autonomy—to build and secure the multidirectional trust and alignment across divisions, departments, geographies, and silos. You need to foster a spirit of confidence, creativity, and appetite for risk to share information, collaborate, and make decisions that benefit the sum of the parts.

In short, it requires you to have a global mindset.

Building a Global Mindset . . . Through a *Cultural* Frame

What is a global mindset? Historically, it was understood to be your ability to work with people and organizations in different countries or cultures. But a global mindset is a little more complex than that.

Yes, a global mindset is about being able to bridge linguistic and societal differences and make collaborations that embrace these differences rather than papering over them. But we believe it is also about understanding that cultural difference goes way beyond nationality.

Culture penetrates every element of our identity—from race and ethnicity to gender, to generation, to political orientation, taste, habits, lived experience, and more. And the cultural differences that manifest among people, groups, and communities involve multiple layers of identity and feelings of belonging that make them much more complex than simply, "Where is this person from and what language do they speak?"[56]

We believe that in a globalized crisis, having a global mindset requires you as a Prepared Leader to think deeply about who you are culturally in relation to other people. And how you and your organization relate to diverse groups or communities across as many dimensions of cultural difference as possible.

That means doing two things.

First, it really does mean understanding the diverse cultural contexts you operate within, both internally and externally. Who are your stakeholders locally and globally? How do issues like race, ethnicity, gender, generational difference, and social or political beliefs shape their values, behaviors, and expectations?

Second, building a global mindset means looking at the crisis in front of you and working through how it might be experienced by these stakeholders—and the implications for them, you, and your organization. It means doing enough scenario planning that integrates these cultural differences, so that you have a strong sense of how your decisions and actions might play out.

You might think this is too much to ask. When you're busy managing the exigencies of a crisis, how can you be expected to factor all this extra complexity into your decision-making?

All you need to do is reflect. Pause and consider what a decision or action might look like to other people with different perspectives—and what the consequences might be.

How do you do this?

Remember that in the previous chapters of this book, we have outlined the different resources and tools that you can prepare now to lead through the next crisis.

We have seen that crises play out across five distinct phases that you can plan for, and that each phase comes with a need for certain leadership competencies that you can develop now.

We have also looked at how you can protect your decision-making from certain biases, from tunnel vision and from the echo chambers that inhibit your ability to see the bigger picture in all its complexity.

We have underscored the importance of diversity—the diversity of perspectives, experience, and expertise within your team or teams. The need to go further, to ask questions, to be willing to surface information from different sources, and to model a culture of curiosity to find multifaceted answers to multifaceted problems.

And we've talked about framing—about our tendency to see crises as threats or opportunities, and how the way that we frame something will influence the way we respond to it.

Let's take another look at how these and some other cultural factors might shape the way that you see the world, interpret crises, and relate to other people—and they to you.

As you read on, think about how things might have evolved differently for CrossFit and Glassman had he paused for reflection and been more purposeful about enacting a global mindset in 2020.

Socio-Cultural Framing: Where You're From

Popular culture is full of stereotypes and caricatures around national identity.

A more scientific approach is to look at what social psychologist Geert Hofstede calls *collective programming*: a set of different attributes or dimensions that can be pronounced in different cultural groups, distinguishing them from one another.[57]

These dimensions include things like how *individualistic* one culture tends to be compared to another or how one culture might prioritize strict power hierarchies while another is more egalitarian. One culture might value *tradition* more than innovation, say; *status quo* over change. And one society may tend to favor the *masculine* virtues of assertiveness and achievement over the *feminine* qualities of cooperation and compassion.

During the pandemic, there was some evidence of how this kind of cultural framing played out in countries with more collective frameworks. In Southeast Asia, for instance, blanket measures like lockdowns were uniformly instituted by countries like Japan at the start of 2020, whereas the United States saw considerable backlash against mask wearing and social distancing—a function of its more individualistic framework.[58]

Generational Framing: How Old You Are

Perhaps one of the most interesting generational divides in the twenty-first century comes in separating Millennials and Generation Z—the digital natives—from older cohorts.

Born into a world that connects them across geographical, national, and cultural fault lines, Millennials and Gen Z are not only more tech savvy, they also appear to be more *heterogeneous* than other generations. Whether they are Asian, African, American, or European, they seem to share certain values, certain perspectives, motivation, and goals. Research and survey data point to their desire for change and strong concern around issues like climate change, social justice, diversity, and global equality of opportunity. They are eager and aggressive, and they have access to knowledge and to digital tools that give them voice and access to power in a way that is unprecedented in previous generations.

The same research suggests that COVID-19 impacted Millennials and Gen Z more negatively than older generations. The economic downturn took more of a toll on these young people, and they reported stronger feelings of anxiety and loneliness during the crisis.[59]

Gender-Based Framing

Gender identity is a complex issue, and it's not part of our remit in this book to talk about this in its fullest dimensions. Briefly, however, we can touch on some of the broadest differences that have emerged between men and women's framing of the COVID-19 crisis.

In October 2020, gender consultant Avivah Wittenberg-Cox published an article in *Harvard Business Review* that explored how the virus had affected countries differently. Those led by women had suffered on average six times fewer confirmed COVID-19 deaths than countries with male heads of state, she found.[60]

Another *HBR* piece, authored by leadership consultants Jack Zenger and Joseph Folkman, found that female business leaders were rated higher than male counterparts across the bulk of leadership competencies during the crisis. Much of this, they said, boiled down to the way women were more adept at delivering *what employees wanted during a crisis.* This included leaders who were able to "pivot and learn new skills; emphasize employee development even when times are tough; display honesty and integrity; and be sensitive and understanding of the stress, anxiety, and frustration that people are feeling," according to Zenger and Folkman's research.[61]

In November 2020, Wittenberg-Cox spoke to the UK's BBC and said of female crisis framing and leadership during the pandemic: "Every smart CEO watches what other leaders do, and I would suggest that what many [men] have done is borrow from the female playbook, which involves being incredibly caring of their stakeholders, and upping their communication skills."[62]

These words recall those of Wonya Lucas, whose story we examined in Chapter 6. For Lucas, taking up the reins at Hallmark in the first wave of the COVID-19 pandemic was less about establishing strategy or vision and more about

getting to that human connection, and tackling the very understandable perceptions of me as an outsider, as someone new. I wanted to convey a very important message: that I was accessible and that I was there for my team during this incredibly difficult time.[63]

We believe Lucas and other Prepared Leaders modeled a female framing during the pandemic—a framing, to quote Wittenberg-Cox, that was *"different in* style and tone" to that of men. But to be clear, not necessarily *better.*

Different crises, different situations call for different types of framing. In a globalized crisis, the onus is on you as a Prepared Leader to locate *yourself* strategically and culturally as you manage *others.*

Ask yourself what cultural factors—what elements of your own identity—might shape the way that you perceive a crisis and influence *your* decisions, as you think about the perspectives, framing mechanisms, and motivations of other individuals, organizations, or communities.

The Globalized Crisis and Mega Communities of Response

There's one more thing to say about globalized crises, and it's tied to a very human tendency to *come together* in adversity.

When we face a collective threat or uncertainty that touches us at an organizational or societal level, human beings often assemble into broad and diverse communities of response. We form conglomerations that are built on a multiformity of knowledge, expertise, and skill. These conglomerates typically transcend differences, bridge silos, and can span organizations, sectors, or even societies. To work, they require structure, communication, and governance. But unlike businesses or government bodies, these conglomerations are unconstrained by rigid hierarchies and as such have an elasticity and agility that can make them more effective at mobilizing in response to crises.

These collectives are known as "mega communities" and are increasingly understood by scholars, business leaders, and governments to have a unique role in tackling some of the biggest problems we collectively face. And they are a force to be reckoned with.[64]

The twenty-first century has some compelling examples of mega communities that have come together to tackle societal issues, enact great change, and reshape global attitudes. One of the great societal phenomena of our times is the #MeToo movement, which began in response to institutionalized sexual harassment and predation in the US film industry but spread to the rest of the world inside of three months, fanned by social and traditional mass media. What started as a tweet in October 2017 amassed a following of more than 17 million social media users almost overnight and was being actively used in 85 countries by the end of the year, when *Time* magazine named the movement its "person of the year." More than 200 powerful individuals and a slew of organizations have felt the force of this social reckoning to date.[65]

The "pandemic era" also has its fair share of mega communities. We've seen how Black Lives Matter built unprecedented momentum around the social justice crisis in the United States and beyond in 2020. Other mega communities sprang up during the COVID-19 crisis. The most famous example is rooted in the human ingenuity to deliver concrete—and game-changing—solutions to arrest its spread.

Vaccines typically take decades of research and testing before they reach the clinic. Yet in 2020, a mega community of scientists, virologists, pharmaceutical companies, government bodies, intergovernmental agencies, and an international army of volunteers—people willing to put their own well-being on the line—developed not one but several effective antidotes to COVID-19.

By February 2021, a little more than a year after the virus first originated, no fewer than 61 vaccines were in human trials around the world. On December 2, the United Kingdom was the first nation to approve the Pfizer- and BioNTech-developed vaccine for mass inoculation. On December 13, the vaccine was approved by the US Food and Drug Administration. It's no small measure of pride to Erika that the mRNA technology on which the Pfizer and Moderna vaccines are based was developed by faculty at the University of Pennsylvania.[66]

Unfortunately, as we know, the story of COVID-19 doesn't end there. Uneven global rollout allowed the virus to mutate in regional hotspots, unleashing successive global waves of new infections into 2021 and 2022. Nonetheless, the mega community of scientists, health bodies, volunteers, and others who developed, tested, and administered vaccines during the peak of the pandemic can be credited with putting together a critical tool in the fight to bring it under control.

The power of the mega community should very much be on the radar of the Prepared Leader, especially in a globalized crisis. When a major crisis hits you and your organization, you need to think about the mechanisms or initiatives that you can deploy to bridge silos, bring diverse groups together, and galvanize mega communities within your organization or ecosystem.

To illustrate that even more, we can turn again to the National Basketball Association's (NBA's) Adam Silver and the National Health Service's (NHS's) Mark Turner.

Silver actively sought cross-functional, extra-organizational input and expertise from a diversity of sources. As the pandemic tightened its grip and the threat to teams and players intensified, this expanded crisis team became a mega community of executives, players, coaches, physiotherapists, health-care experts, and others who together created an Orlando "bubble"—an NBA "city" that demonstrated to the world that businesses with strict testing and safety protocols could operate and thrive in the pandemic.

Similarly, when Turner invited London's physicians to ideate a solution to patient backlogs, he and his colleagues paved the way for a mega community of executive staff, surgeons, doctors, nurses, and health-care providers to simultaneously work through non-COVID procedures, all the time bracing for a new wave of infections.

In our own experience leading town-hall meetings and cross-silo task forces, we have seen faculty, staff, students, and sometimes alumni come together in new collaborations, sharing knowledge, deferring to expertise, innovating, and problem-solving even as COVID-19 closed our campuses and drove unprecedented, comprehensive shifts to online teaching, learning, and communicating.

Technology had a huge role to play in facilitating the work and the accomplishments of the many mega communities that came together in the "pandemic era." Our capacity to use science and technology—to apply tools of our own design to the most complex challenges we face—is a function of the questing intelligence, the inventiveness and integrity that human beings have in the face of adversity.

In the next chapter, we take a deeper look at how we use technology in a globalized crisis, as well as at the opportunities and risks that need to be on your radar as a Prepared Leader.

Takeaways for Prepared Leaders

- In a globalized crisis, Prepared Leaders will need a global mindset to manage crises locally and globally—and be cognizant of the threats and opportunities that exist in different operational and cultural contexts.

- A global mindset is far more than sensitivity to societal differences.

- A truly global mindset integrates the cultural and contextual differences that shape worldview and anticipates how these differences might play out in globalized crises.

- In a globalized crisis, human beings tend to form mega communities that transcend expertise, silos, and organizations, to respond to challenges.

- Prepared Leaders should think about how to facilitate their own mega communities of response, within and beyond their organizations.

Chapter 8

Technology and Crises

Technology is an enabler. It is not the end solution.
—Lubomila Jordanova, CEO, Plan A

Technology undoubtedly contributed to the spread of COVID-19 in early 2020 as human beings moved without restriction, from country to country, on planes, trains, cars, and cruise ships. But without technology, the devastation wrought by the pandemic would have been incalculably worse.

Digital and social media channels kept information pumping around the planet almost as quickly as the spread of disease itself, enabling leaders everywhere to see the emerging signs and take measures to brace for impact.

Next-generation technologies like AI and blockchain were used to track and trace infection and to fortify supply chains as a function of international preparatory and preventive efforts. Meanwhile, 3-D printing accelerated the production of personal protective equipment for frontline workers and ventilators for the gravely ill, while scientists deployed the latest in gene editing, synthetic biology, and nanotechnologies to develop diagnostics, treatments, and vaccines at record speed. Telehealth technologies were key to containing the damage and limiting the spread of COVID-19, as a means of routing severe cases to hospitals but keeping mild instances isolated at home.

Recognition must also go to the likes of Zoom, Microsoft Teams, Skype, and other technologies that kept learners, educators, employees, and businesses connected. Those technologies helped accelerate a globalized shift to online learning and working that might otherwise have taken a decade or more to happen. Similarly, the digital technologies that powered businesses like ridesharing before the pandemic were used by enterprising firms to switch to food and supplies delivery, which simultaneously helped keep organizations afloat, salaries paid, and households fed. It all helped pave the way not only for recovery, but also for some businesses and sectors to emerge better than before the crisis.

What COVID-19 has to teach Prepared Leaders is that in our modern world, technology is a critical tool you can deploy across the different phases of crisis management. You can use technology to significantly enhance and extend your ability to detect the signs, brace for impact, prevent or contain damage, and accelerate your recovery. Technology can also be instrumental in learning from a crisis and in informing the systems and processes, culture, and behaviors that will fortify you and your organization for the crises to come.

But there's something else to say about technology: *Technology is only as good as the leader who uses it.*

Technology: Risk or Opportunity? Friend or Foe?

The pandemic era has plenty of examples of Prepared Leaders who optimized technology to change the course of a crisis for themselves and their organizations and to build toward a better future.

For Turner of the UK's National Health Service (NHS) London, the pandemic was a chance to experiment with collaboration technology as a means of expediting problem-solving under pressure. This yielded new ways of working that were not only more effective but more inclusive.

"The pandemic obliged us to use new technologies like Microsoft Teams to stay in touch," he told us. "What we discovered is that with Teams, you can run *hackathons*—short bursts of collaborative, team-based problem-solving—meaning we could bring people together from across the organizational matrix to focus on specific challenges, such as the recovery of breast screens or endoscopy services."

Turner used hackathons to bring in a diversity of perspective and defer to or leverage expertise. And it is a practice that he describes as a "playbook" for rapid problem-solving, and one that he hopes will combat the "regulatory complexity that can ossify systems such as public health care."

Turner continued, "The situation gave us more leeway to make critical decisions fast and to do what we thought was right and best in the context. We cut through a lot of red tape as a result and followed needs as the crisis has dictated. The challenge will be to lock in the benefits of some of the changes we have made in the longer-term. But if we can demonstrate the value of this kind of flexibility and agile decision-making and back that up with evidence, then we have a better chance of formalizing this kind of change and continuing to cut through red tape going forward."[67]

In a crisis, technology can be your friend. But it can also be your foe. In the last chapter, we took a brief look at the case of CrossFit's Greg Glassman. Glassman made ill-judged use of Twitter at the height of the social justice reckoning in June 2020.

Glassman's tweet—his first public statement about the Floyd murder—appeared amid growing public outrage and a demand for businesses to show support for social justice. It came as the cumulative positive cases of COVID-19 in the United States were approaching 1.7 million.[68]

The backlash was as fierce as it was immediate. Criticism of the CrossFit CEO and calls for him to resign began trending across the Twittersphere and remained unquelled by the time Glassman tweeted an apology. But things were about to get worse for him and for CrossFit.

The same day his Twitter apology appeared, internet media company BuzzFeed reported a slew of racially inflammatory remarks Glassman had made to affiliated gym owners on a Zoom conference call. This call had been set up at the behest of CrossFit gyms and staff looking to understand the company's position on the social justice crisis. Glassman was recorded telling these stakehold-ers that he was "not mourning for George Floyd" simply because this was the "white thing to do." In the same recording, he went on to share several conspiracy theories around the origin of the pandemic and urged gym owners to "pretend to comply" with health restric-tions when gyms reopened.[69]

Hundreds of CrossFit gyms instantly cut their ties with the com-pany. Reebok rescinded its nine-year sponsorship of the brand, and a number of high-profile athletes took to social media to announce they would no longer be CrossFit ambassadors. By June 10, Glassman announced he would step down as CEO and that he would be sell-ing the company. It had taken three days, one Zoom call, and a three-word tweet to bring down one of the most disruptive and successful players in the fitness industry.

What do the diverging examples of Turner and Glassman have to tell us about Prepared Leadership, technology, and crises? *Technology is only as good as the leader who uses it.*

Digital tools are instruments you can deploy with enormous effect to see the signs, brace for impact, contain damage, build toward recovery, and expedite learning from the experience to prepare for the next crisis.

But unless you prioritize the other dimensions of Prepared Leadership, these powerful tools also have the potential to make things worse for you and your organization. What are those dimen-sions? Let's recap.

Turner and Glassman's stories both illustrate in different ways the critical importance of sense-making and perspective-taking—among the critical nine skills that Prepared Leaders must deploy in a crisis, as we saw in Chapter 3.

Both stories speak to the need to defend rational decision-making under pressure, and guard against the hardwired heuristics or cognitive biases that can impair judgment. And they remind us to be mindful of the framing mechanisms that we looked at in Chapter 4—mechanisms that condition how we see a crisis as a threat or opportunity and shape the decisions we make in response.

These stories also speak to the importance of diversity in your team, as we saw in Chapters 5 and 6, and its role in accessing the further reaches of your organization and stakeholder ecosystem, to surface information that will enrich your decision-making.

And they illustrate just how very important it is to develop the understanding and the mindset to manage crises that are at once local and globalized—the *global mindset* that makes you sensitive to the cultural and contextual differences that shape the way your diverse stakeholders experience a crisis.

How do you integrate these dimensions of Prepared Leadership into your own leadership practice? By seeking out a diversity of perspective, knowledge, insight, and expertise. By acknowledging and leveraging expertise wherever it surfaces. By building the processes and systems that allow information to flow through your organization and inform your understanding. By asking questions, listening, and reflecting on your own biases and framing mechanisms.

Another element of the CrossFit story underscores the importance.

On June 3, the owner of an affiliated gym, Alyssa Royse, wrote a letter that reached Glassman's desk. That letter announced that Rocket Community Fitness would be disaffiliating itself from CrossFit because of the company's silence on the Floyd murder. In a response also made public, Glassman accused Royse of being "a really shitty person" and suggested that the pandemic had affected her mental health. For Royse, and countless other affiliates and partners, Glassman's reaction was unfathomable. As she put it: "The irony is that my letter was an attempt to say, 'Hey, I think there is danger ahead,' precisely to avoid exactly what is now happening."[70]

In our hyper-connected, always-on world, where information flows seamlessly and in real time, the powerful tools of social media can add layers of complexity to crisis management.

We have developed a tool for Prepared Leaders that builds on the nine competencies for crisis management that we looked at in Chapter 3. This tool uses the lens of social media to pinpoint some opportunities you will have as a Prepared Leader to build effective crisis management skills before, during, and after a crisis. The tool can be found at our website we referenced in this book's introduction, https://jamesandwooten.com.[71]

Paradigm Shifts and Predictive Possibilities

Technology, used judiciously, can be an extraordinary tool in crisis management.

In the pandemic era, as we have seen, technology helped us brace for the impact of COVID-19 and contain much of its damage. It helped us preserve and maintain much of our business operations even when people and organizations were in lockdown, which in turn helped us recover. And we also used technology to learn—to devise new ways to accelerate some of the most transformational trends in our key industries.

In her talks with leaders, Lynn often refers to the "Three H's" of hospitality, health care, and higher education. The latter is, of course, very close to our personal experience. In the pandemic era, Prepared Leaders were able to use technology to effectively drive a paradigm shift across these three industries—sectors that have historically been slow to transform.

At the start of this chapter, we touched on some of this transformation. In health care and hospitality, Prepared Leaders were able to use technology to make COVID-19 a catalyst for change. From telemedicine to digitally driven diagnostics to automated patient care; from app-enabled delivery of food and supplies to the Restaurant of Tomorrow, change was served up in the first few months of the pandemic at a rate faster than all other corporate accelerators together. All of it was made possible by digital tools.[72]

In our field, technology kept us connected to our learning communities during COVID-19. We also used technology to advance a new era of online learning, virtual learning, and blended or hybrid learning. This integrates a plethora of platforms and mechanisms, from synchronous video sessions to holograms, to podcasts and interactive media, to virtual field trips, engaging learners of all types in new ways. Our hope is the gains we are seeing in access and inclusion and in creative learning and innovation will continue to gather pace.

Our colleague Mauro Guillén, dean of Cambridge Judge Business School, is an authority on global market trends. Looking at the pandemic era, he sees evidence of Prepared Leaders making excellent use of digital resources to build organizational agility and resilience while also using the crisis as an opportunity to rethink—and prepare for—the future.

"The pandemic simultaneously gave businesses an imperative to stop, to recalibrate, and to reset towards a better future, while throwing up a host of inter-connected internal and external challenges that are as urgent as they are existential," Guillén said. "To rise to these challenges, forward-thinking CEOs began using technological tools in different ways. These trends have gathered pace and momentum in the pandemic's wake, and they should be something for leaders in all kinds of organizations and sectors to consider."

Artificial intelligence (AI) and machine learning had been gaining traction in businesses before the pandemic for two predominant reasons, Guillén said: to fortify supply chains through intelligent inventory planning, management, and procurement; and to better understand customer behaviors and usage patterns. Interestingly, in the wake of COVID-19, these technologies are increasingly being deployed as forecasting mechanisms.

After COVID-19, more progressive leaders have prioritized the need to plan for the next big thing—the next disruption, crisis, or opportunity. These leaders are looking to the pattern recognition capabilities of machine learning and AI to understand not only the probability of something happening in two or three years, but to capture the specificities of what that thing or next crisis will be to prepare to manage them now.

Prepared Leaders are using technology to pinpoint the kinds of capabilities they will need to develop—both internally and by bringing in risk consultants—to manage the next major disruption ahead, says Guillén. AI and big data can help distinguish the signs from the noise, as well as make sense of those signs.[73]

Plan A is a small business that Lubomila Jordanova founded in 2017. It uses big data and AI to pinpoint climate-related risks to enterprises and tailor plans that manage and mitigate that risk. The company has gained extraordinary traction during the pandemic era, Jordanova said, as leaders increasingly understand that climate risk is financial risk—and that risk can be existential.

"Business strategy has historically been tied to KPIs [key performance indicators] around financial performance and regulatory shifts," Jordanova said. "Now, with the climate crisis unfolding around us, leaders are seeing they need to do far more to prepare their organizations for the *unintended costs* that come with the disruption, the catastrophes, that are associated with climate change."[74]

These costs are increasing quickly, she says, growing at a rate of 6% year over year. In 2021, insurance group Swiss Re estimated that insured losses due to natural disasters came to $112 billion globally—the fourth highest amount on record.[75] Jordanova stated,

What we're doing is using big data to rate companies' performance relative to climate risk across factors like carbon emissions and their geographical operations. And we use AI to identify the actions they need to take now—including the reporting they need to do to mitigate regulatory risk—as well as the cost to them of inaction or failing to prepare.

Firms that fail to prepare for climate change are exposed to risks not only in terms of natural disaster, supply chain disruption, and regulatory penalties, but also around things like recruitment, access to capital investment, and loss of revenue. Yet, as Guillén noted, COVID-19 has provided considerable impetus—an opportunity—for Prepared Leaders to turn to technology to brace for future crises. Plan A has been "positively overwhelmed by demand" in the wake of the pandemic, Jordanova says.

The pandemic, she believes, has left organizations more concerned about how prepared they are for the future. And at the same time "more alive to the possibilities" that technology offers to optimize procedures.

It's worth noting that the Plan A founder, like us, sees technology very much as an "enabler," and not an end.

Prepared Leaders can use technology to help them detect the signs, make sense of information, brace for impact, contain damage, drive their recovery, and learn from the experience. Technology can help pinpoint risk, determine necessary actions, and monitor the results. And it can facilitate decision-making, communications, stakeholder management, operations management, the delivery of your services and products, and the enablement of your culture.

Technology helped Prepared Leaders like the NHS's Turner and Hallmark's Lucas to bring diversity into the room and to access the different perspectives and knowledge—the expertise from across the organizational hierarchy that made a critical difference when COVID-19 disrupted business and threatened to overrun the NHS.

But again, technology is only as good as the Prepared Leader who uses it. Leveraging technology in a crisis also fundamentally entails understanding that it is a tool that can be used for change—but just a tool, nonetheless—and that digital transformation ultimately is people transformation.

In a crisis, your use of technology will be shaped by your ability to educate, mobilize, include, and align your people. Your success in leveraging digital tools will be contingent on how well you make sense of the situation and how well you frame it; the speed and effectiveness of your decision-making, and its ethical dimensions; how inclusive your leadership is of all your stakeholders, internal and external; the transparency of your communication; and how much you prioritize diversity of opinion, perspective, and expertise.

In short, how well you use technology in the next crisis will depend on how well you understand and enact the tenets of Prepared Leadership.

Of course, no chapter on technology and crises can be complete without acknowledging that there are always actors in a crisis who will not be able to benefit from digital resources.

In the COVID-19 crisis, frontline workers in health care, supply chains, food and medicine production, and logistics were not afforded the kind of protection that employees in other sectors were able to enjoy. Those people whose jobs could not be done remotely were subject to greater risk of infection at the height of the pandemic, as they continued to work outside the home to earn a living. It's estimated that in the United States, only 16% of blue-collar workers were able to work virtually, compared to just under half of their white-collar counterparts. One survey undertaken by US employment website Joblist reported that this demographic also suffered a significantly higher percentage of layoffs than office-based, or "skilled," workers—66% to 40%, respectively.[76]

COVID-19 has plenty to teach us still—about commonality and difference; about inequity and injustice in our communities, as well as about the shared vulnerabilities to crises that define our globalized economy and interconnected world.

COVID-19 has much to teach us about the utility of the tools that we have at our disposal—tools of our own making that can expedite solutions almost beyond our imagining; technologies that can bring us together even when we must be apart; and technologies that have the power to transform the way we communicate, work, live, and get things done under the most extraordinary pressure. But it also shows us that those tools are only as good as the leader who puts them to use. Above all, COVID-19 teaches us something critical about the *agency of leadership*—how it is within our power to shape outcomes for better or for worse, and how we can lead through a crisis even more effectively, if we are truly prepared.

The lessons of the pandemic are manifold. But they are meaningless unless we are prepared to do the one thing that is absolutely required of us. And that is *to learn*.

Takeaways for Prepared Leaders

- Technology can provide powerful solutions to challenges in a crisis.

- However, technology can also make things significantly worse if misused.

- In a crisis, technology is only as good as the leader who uses it.

- The tenets of Prepared Leadership outlined, chapter by chapter, in this book will help you prepare to use technology effectively when the next crisis strikes.

Chapter 9

Learning and the Prepared Leader

It would be foolish for us not to try to learn from
everything that's happening.
—Adam Silver, commissioner,
National Basketball Association

We began this book looking at what the World Bank's Jim Yong Kim so presciently described as the "cycles of panic and neglect" that stymie all our efforts to prepare for crises.

In each successive chapter, we have outlined a framework built around the agency of leadership—a group of attitudes, skills, and actions—that can help us break these cycles of panic and neglect. Collectively, we call this Prepared Leadership. Our aim in writing this book has been to explain to you exactly what we mean by Prepared Leadership and how you can develop and adopt these attitudes, skills, and actions to become a Prepared Leader yourself.

In this chapter, we want to stress something critical: You cannot prepare for any future crisis without first *learning the lessons that experience has to teach.*

Your capacity to prepare for what lies beyond the next crisis is only as good as your ability to learn from the lessons it shares. In this sense, Prepared Leadership is essentially about learning.

At its core, Prepared Leadership is your willingness to learn and to convert learning into action, because if you don't identify the lessons of today's crisis and integrate those lessons in your decision-making, framing mechanisms, and your processes and practice as a leader, you leave yourself and your organization vulnerable to the crisis of tomorrow. You risk falling into the cycles of panic and neglect that we see over and over again.

In Chapter 2 of this book, we outlined the five phases of crisis management. These five phases form a continuum—an uninterrupted and recurring sequence of actions we perform to remain constantly prepared for whatever's next. Learning is embedded throughout.

As one crisis recedes, even as one phase of crisis management is completed, we learn from the experience to better execute our continuing cycle, which involves the following steps:

1. Early warning and signal detection
2. Preparation and prevention
3. Damage containment
4. Recovery
5. Learning and reflection

In this final chapter, we look at learning. We look at what stops us from learning and what we stand to lose. We look at how we learn—from others, from experience—and how learning is a key gateway in seeing the opportunities that crises yield. And we ask you some important questions as we go—questions that we hope will give you pause to reflect on how you and your organization learn.

Finally, we share some very concrete takeaways for Prepared Leaders that will help you and your organization learn before, during, and after a crisis.

First, let's look at how and why decision-makers, leaders, and organizations fail to learn.

Failure to Learn

Why is Adam Silver often cited as an example of good leadership during the pandemic era, whereas CrossFit's Greg Glassman's fate became something of a cautionary tale? Neither leader's business was new to crises when COVID-19 struck.

The National Basketball Association (NBA) has been rocked by a raft of scandals in recent years, among them accusations of discrimination and racism against team owners and domestic violence against players. Yet Silver has been praised for his effective management of each crisis.

The issue of domestic violence has shaken up other sports in recent years, particularly the National Football League (NFL) in the United States. In 2014, Silver said,

> We learn from other leagues' experiences. We're studying everything that's been happening in the NFL. The whole world's focused right now on what's happening around the NFL, so it would be foolish for us not to try to learn from everything that's happening.[77]

When an NBA player was convicted of assaulting a woman in a hotel the same year, he was immediately suspended. The NBA also published what one media outlet called "a thorough piece of literature, documenting exactly what happened, exactly who knew about it, exactly how the league proceeded."[78]

In this public statement, Silver listed the names of every adviser whose counsel he had sought—a diverse group that included lawmakers, domestic violence experts, and nongovernmental organizations (NGOs) as well as different members of the NBA leadership team.[79]

What does this tell you about Silver's leadership in terms of learning?

Now let's look at Glassman. The George Floyd–related controversy was not the first time that CrossFit had fallen out of public favor on social media. Only two years previously, in 2018, the company attracted fierce criticism when a senior executive, Russell Berger, seemingly endorsed anti–Gay Pride sentiments on Twitter. "Pride is a sin," Berger wrote, drawing immediate backlash. It even elicited this response from Glassman:

He needs to take a big dose of "shut the f— up" and hide out for a while. We do so much good work with such pure hearts—to have some zealot in his off-time do something this stupid, we're all upset.

Within 48 hours, Berger was fired.

Glassman made those remarks on June 6, 2018. Exactly two years later, his "Floyd-19" tweet appeared. We can infer that he failed to learn the lessons of a crisis, in this case about discrimination, reputation, and the dangers of social media.[80]

There's some indication that the culture of CrossFit under Glassman's leadership was prone to discrimination, sexual harassment from the top down, and a command-and-control approach that had created a corporate environment governed by "fear." The *New York Times* ran a piece citing workers who described CrossFit as a "sexist company culture."[81] One former employee said Glassman had "ruled by a fear of retribution that kept subordinates in line."[82]

We believe leaders who fail to learn from experience fail in four key ways:[83]

1. **Failure to scan:** leaders who fail to understand that crises happen again and again. Failure to scan, to spot the signs and prepare, leaves you vulnerable to the next crisis, even if you weather this one.
2. **Failure to make sense:** leaders who fail to pull together different sources of information to see the bigger picture, who are too narrow in their vision or understanding, and who seek confirmation instead of challenging their assumptions.
3. **Failure to seek out diverse perspectives:** leaders who fail to empower and incentivize their people to share critical insight or expertise and prioritize the flow of information around the organization.
4. **Failure to determine critical lessons:** leaders who fail to draw the lessons from previous experience and use those lessons to

improve processes and systems going forward—the very processes that will safeguard scanning, sense-making, and the seeking out of diverse perspectives.

What is it that drives these behaviors? What sets leaders up to fail to learn in these ways?

We believe there are three root causes—three principal barriers to learning that make it more difficult for you and your organization to learn efficiently, to embed learning, and to use it to fortify your resources in times of crisis:

1. Leading a culture that is discriminatory and/or lacking in diversity
2. Using framing mechanisms that set the wrong goals
3. Becoming complacent about the possibility of crises happening

In our research over the years, we've looked at several organizations that have allowed discriminatory cultures to flourish. What happens to these organizations in times of crisis?

First, where people don't speak up; where they are scared to share different perspectives or surface information that might be important; where a diversity of expertise and insight is neither valued nor proactively sought out but crushed, organizations will struggle to spot the signs, brace for impact, manage the damage, and recover. But in terms of learning from the experience, they are also on the back foot.

Where discrimination and a lack of diversity flourish, so too do short-sighted leadership, myopic leadership, and echo chambers. Worse still, these are organizations that usually become defensive in the context of a crisis. Blame is all too often externalized—apportioned to others, to victims in cases of discrimination or harassment. Leaders deny responsibility. The problem with this kind of culture is that it actively blocks learning. It quells curiosity about what underlying causes there might be—what organizational norms or procedures might contribute to crises, make you vulnerable to them, or even cause them to happen.

In failing to take steps to learn and to determine root causes internally as well as externally, you miss an opportunity to address issues within your organization, your culture, and your leadership. As a result, you are vulnerable to the same issues and the same kinds of crises down the line.

Similarly, the way you frame a crisis will have a huge effect (right or wrong) on goals you set for your organization in terms of managing it over the short and long terms.

In Chapter 4, we looked at the way we tend to frame crises as threats, not opportunities, while in reality they are both. If your framing is exclusively around crises as a threat, it's likely your objectives will be short term and urgent. You will want to neutralize that threat, put out the fires, and get back to business as normal as quickly as possible. Containment and recovery are critical phases of crisis management, but so too is learning. In framing a crisis exclusively as a threat, you risk missing the critical opportunity to learn from it—to pause and dig deep into internal and external issues that you need to address, and to use that learning to build your understanding and resilience in front of the challenges and crises that are waiting down the line.

Now let's look at complacency in more depth.

The Complacency Barrier and Vicarious Learning

Crises are rare events. They are recurrent, but they're also infrequent. Many of you will never have faced an accusation of discrimination or domestic abuse within your workforce. You may never have had a colleague ill-advisedly speak out on a culturally sensitive issue. Your experience of crisis might be limited.

Similarly, it's easy to see crises as events that happen to other people. In Chapters 1 and 4, we looked at human cognitive biases that affect the way we see threat and that impair our decision-making. We talked about *probability neglect, hyperbolic discounting, confirmation bias*—hardwired beliefs that keep us moving forward in a dangerous and uncertain world because essentially we're convinced that whatever it is, it won't happen to us.

Lack of experience coupled with cognitive bias can make us complacent about crises. And complacency is another barrier to learning.

But just because something hasn't happened (yet) doesn't mean it won't happen. And simply because you have not had firsthand experience of a crisis, it doesn't mean you cannot learn from the experience of others.

Recall what Silver said about learning from the NFL experience to prepare for the threat of NBA players charged with domestic violence. Prepared Leaders routinely document policies, strategies, and paradigms—from inside and outside the organization.

We look to the experience of others to flesh out our own (in)experience and augment our understanding of the issues—the crises—that might befall us. Analyzing and benchmarking what others do—be they competitors, regulators, policymakers, or leaders in organizations, industries, and sectors other than our own—is a chance to learn *vicariously*. Vicarious learning is critical.

Kristy Towry is professor of accounting at Goizueta Business School at Emory University and an authority on learning and decision-making. With fellow researchers Willie Choi, Gary Hecht, and Ivo Tafkov, she has run laboratory experiments that look at how humans learn through others. She said:

In our experiments, we have people look at third-party case studies with successful and less successful outcomes, and we also have them watch other participants try to solve puzzles. What we find over and over is that vicarious learning really broadens the way people understand a problem in all its complexity and helps them make decisions that are less tactical and more strategic.[84]

When we limit our understanding of a problem or situation to our own experience alone, we become *myopic* about the wider context. We prioritize what's happening in the immediate here and now, and neglect to think about past causes or future outcomes, Towry says. Our learning is limited.

"When there's a lot of background noise or complexity to manage in a decision-making situation, looking at other people's experience or behaviors actually helps us determine the bigger picture and discernible patterns to make better sense of it," she said.

Then there's the value of learning from other people's failures as opposed to their successes. And this is a little more complex, Hecht says.

"Human beings prefer success to failure. When someone succeeds at something, we want to copy what they do to emulate their success. In our experiments, participants typically focus their learning on the success of others—they meticulously record the decisions and steps they take to solve a problem or a puzzle. But when they look at instances of failure, they tend to focus on the broader patterns or general things that led to less favorable outcomes," he told us.

In a crisis setting, focusing on the specifics of people's successes won't be so helpful because crises are usually unique events that cannot be exactly replicated, says Hecht.

You're actually better off looking at similar instances where someone has failed to get something done and use this kind of broader stroke learning for insights into what you might want to do—or not want to do. In a crisis, there's a strong argument for looking at the *forest* rather than the *trees*.

Vicarious learning, and learning from other people's failures, is a powerful tool to overcome complacency and lack of experience when a crisis hits. But isn't it too much of an ask when you're managing the immediacy of a crisis to put down tools and start hunting for other people's experience?

"You need to enable learning before a crisis hits you," Towry says.

Ask yourself these questions: How do you enable vicarious learning within your organization—and within your own leadership practice? Whose leadership and decision-making do you reference as a source of learning, and how routinely do you do so? Do you limit your benchmarking to within your own organization or sector, or do you scan for learning opportunities in other spheres? And how do you document the insights you glean?

As a Prepared Leader, it falls to you to build the culture, the processes, mechanisms, and infrastructure within your organization that is geared to collaborative, shared—and vicarious—learning, before, during, and after a crisis.

Learning *Before, During,* and *After* a Crisis

Throughout this book, we have sought to convey several critical ideas. Among them is the notion that crises *always happen*. They are unusual and they are infrequent, but they are inevitable. The core idea that we want to share with you is that to fully leverage your agency as a leader to direct the impact of a crisis and shape better outcomes for you and your organization, you need to be prepared.

Being a Prepared Leader, we have argued, is built upon understanding that crises are inevitable and that they happen across a lifespan of five different phases—phases that you can proactively manage if you develop the supporting skills and competencies. Being prepared means guarding against certain biases and frameworks, cognitive traps that impair your decision-making. And doing this successfully entails broadening your perspective; championing diversity, knowledge, and expertise wherever it surfaces in your organization; and building a team that mirrors these values. Being prepared means using technology judiciously, and it means understanding that in our complex, interconnected world, crises can become globalized—and what to do when that happens.

Perhaps most of all, being a Prepared Leader means being disposed to learn and creating a learning orientation within your organization. It means setting up the systems and the protocols to capture learning at an individual and systemic level—and convert that learning into your systems and processes. How do you do this?

There are certain things that you can do across the five phases of crisis management: before, during, and after a crisis. Now, this might feel counterintuitive to you, especially during a crisis, when you are in the thick of things—preventing a crisis from unfolding or working to contain its damage. But learning is still a critical dimension of being a Prepared Leader at each phase. It's just up to you to make it happen.

These are the things that we believe you need to prioritize.

As you read on, think about your organization in the context of COVID-19. And try to think too about your organization in the context of the next crisis that you are likely to experience, particularly because of any changes that the pandemic has caused for you.

Before a Crisis: Early Warnings, Signal Detection, and Prevention

This is when you need to drive a *culture of learning and reflection* that includes constant analysis of successes and failures (yours and others) and systemic issues that could lead to a crisis. Ask yourself and your team:

- How can you make this a day-to-day business process or function, and who needs to be involved?
- As you go through scenario planning, are there opportunities for vicarious learning from other leaders, organizations, or industries?
- How will you capture information that surfaces and integrate it into decision-making?
- How will you determine any actions that need to be taken and by whom?

This is also when you should make time to assess your team or organization's capabilities and determine learning needs. Ask yourself and your team:

- How can you accurately determine any needs or shortfalls, and what additional input do you need?
- What kind of learning plan might you need in terms of targets, format, and frequency?
- How will you measure success here?

Before a crisis is when you also need to start prioritizing the nine leadership competencies outlined in Chapter 3. Ask yourself and your team how you can accelerate the following:

- Sense-making
- Perspective-taking
- Influence
- Organizational agility
- Creativity
- Communicating effectively
- Risk-taking
- Promoting resilience
- Individual and systemic learning

During a Crisis: Damage Containment and Driving Recovery

Even as you are in full crisis-management mode, you need to remain open to every opportunity to surface information and to learn from as many diverse stakeholders exposed to the crisis as possible, to minimize impact and accelerate recovery. Ask yourself and your team:

- Who (else) can you learn from: Whose perspective or expertise can shed important light on this crisis, and are

there any players within or external to your organization
who can augment your knowledge and understanding?
- If people are unwilling or feel unable to speak up, what can
you do to include them?
- Should circumstances change fast, what barriers might there
be to innovation, risk-taking, or experimentation, and how
can you overcome them?

After a Crisis: Recovery, Learning, and Reflection

As the crisis abates, you will want to focus efforts on putting together
a post-crisis review to capture the lessons and translate them into
concrete takeaways for the future. Ask yourself and your team:

- Who will you assemble among your stakeholders to include
in your post-crisis review, and what are the questions you
need to ask: How might you have done things differently to
achieve different outcomes?
- How will you ensure that failure as well as success becomes a
learning opportunity?
- How will you determine, document, and share the lessons
and takeaways of this crisis, and what actions will you
take to drive necessary change in your culture, systems, or
processes?

Your post-crisis review is also a time to think about ways to build
recovery and resilience among your workforce. As a Prepared Leader,
you will need to find ways to acknowledge that learning and growth
has happened, to recognize the stretch effort that people will
have made, and to drive a culture where people are encouraged to
experiment and learn and rewarded when they create and share
knowledge.

This is also the moment to think about ways to develop emotional intelligence in tandem with other, technical skills and to
foment a sense of optimism and possibility such that your teams and

workforce feel buoyed to see crisis—the next crisis—as an *opportunity*, just as much as a risk.[85]

Learning How to See Crisis as an Opportunity

We started this book by saying that crises can be leveraged to drive organizational change and unlock future innovation, and we have returned to the idea that crises are risks *and* opportunities throughout.

Crises are opportunities to learn. They can help enact organizational change and revitalization precisely because they can shed important light on practices or processes, weaknesses, or cultural problems—vulnerabilities that lead to a smoldering crisis or make you and your organization all the more susceptible to globalized crises in our interconnected world. They are also opportunities to pause and to reset, as we saw in Chapter 8—to leverage technology to build new solutions, greater resilience, and the predictive capabilities to brace for whatever is likely to happen next. The pandemic era has provided a plethora of examples, seen throughout this book, of organizations that have used the COVID-19 crisis as an opportunity to consolidate their reputation or their competitive position, or even to pivot into new spaces and markets.

But this is only possible if you and your organization transition from the anxiety, anger, or despair that crises can entail, to an outlook of optimism and hope. And you cannot do this without learning—without having the courage and the curiosity to unroot the causes, explore the reasons, surface the information, and channel all of this into new ways to strengthen your organization and its environment and to refocus your capabilities. You cannot do any of this unless you ask questions and embrace answers.

We believe learning is at the very core of being a Prepared Leader.

We believe learning is what will empower you to fully leverage your agency to spot the signs of the next crisis coming your way, be ready for it, minimize the damage it might cause, and accelerate your recovery into new opportunities. Learning is at the core of your ability as a Prepared Leader to break the cycles of panic and neglect that left so many of us so very vulnerable to COVID-19.

We live in extraordinary times. These are times of huge risk and uncertainty. The promise of crisis is greater for people, organizations, and societies than at any other moment in our recent past. Geopolitical tensions, trade wars, global debt, inequality, social justice and racial divides, and the great harm done by the pandemic to education, mental health, to the prospects of our younger generations—these are just some of the storms that are gathering on our horizons. Engulfing it all are the changes happening to the natural world that threaten life as we know it: our biodiversity, the air that we breathe, the water we drink, the food we eat, and the very places that we call home.

It's tempting to give up and resign ourselves to the inevitable. But we don't believe that is an option. We believe that human beings are imperfect, prone to mistakes and erroneous beliefs, and often slow to change. But we also believe that human beings have an extraordinary capacity to learn, to adapt and pivot, to find new solutions to new problems, to deploy the great gifts of creativity and invention, and to forge ahead of adversity to build a better world for us all.

Crises will always happen. So too will moments of great discovery and astonishing accomplishment. The key is to be ready for it all. The key is to be prepared.

We began this book by telling you that Prepared Leadership needs to be your fourth bottom line. Prepared Leadership is what will determine your ability to lead through the next crisis and to protect the needs of people, planet, and profit when the unthinkable happens again. Prepared Leadership is the one determinant that will help you navigate uncertainty—even chaos—in order to shape better outcomes and a better outlook for you and your organization.

As we start to look toward the future, we want to stress that being prepared depends on *you*. It is your responsibility as a leader. It is up to you to internalize what you now know about crises, the risk of neglect after panic, and your own agency—*your power* to influence events, to achieve better results, and to forge a better future. It falls to you to put into place the systems, processes, and culture to manage the next crisis inclusively, ethically, and effectively—and to model that culture.

Finally, it is up to you to use every tool at your disposal to make this happen. This book is a tool. By reading it, you have taken a decisive step toward becoming a fully Prepared Leader.

Conclusion
What's Next?

The Prepared Leader marks a significant shift in our thinking and in the way we frame crisis leadership as scholars. Writing this book has helped us bring all this into focus at a time when the world has faced one of the greatest crises in living memory. Publishing this book as the world began to emerge from the depths of the pandemic era and immediately into another global, geopolitical crisis—the war in Ukraine—underscores one of the core ideas that has taken deep hold in our thinking over time and that forms part of the central premise of *The Prepared Leader*: Crises are never one-off events.

They happen again and again and again, although we never seem to expect them. The second idea we set out in this book is that we can prepare for crises. We can prepare ourselves as leaders, and we can prepare our teams and our people, processes, and systems to withstand the shock and "bounce forward."

In this book, we have set out this new framing of crisis leadership in detail. We have looked at the hardwired psychological biases that make all of us vulnerable to crises and the cycles of panic and neglect that exemplify our collective response to shocks like COVID-19. From there, we've talked about what crises are, how they develop across five distinct phases, and the skills that you will need to develop and deploy at each phase to lead yourself and your team through to the next. We've taken a deep dive into the dynamics of your decision-making, which will be tested again and again by the urgency, the unpredictability, and the emotional stress of the crisis situation, and we've shared techniques that will bolster your analytical thinking when disaster strikes.

And we've told you that you cannot lead through a crisis alone. You will need the full support of an empowered and diverse team with boots on the ground and eyes everywhere. A critical idea we want you to take away is that diversity matters. In a crisis, you will need a broad palette of expertise, perspective, and experience in order to surface information, understand the dimensions of what you're dealing with, and entrust the right people with the right responsibilities. Trust, too, is a core idea that we've tried to share with you—the importance of swift bidirectional trust and the need for a certain vulnerability for that trust to take root.

In the final chapters of this book, we've seen how crises can be all engulfing in our globalized world, and we've tried to frame what we mean by adopting a global mindset—the ability to understand yourself in relation to other people, other stakeholders, and other cultures as you grapple with the multidimensional exigencies of a globalized crisis. And in the same context, we've looked at digital technology—both friend and potential foe in a crisis—and we've invited you to think about how technology is only as good as the Prepared Leader who uses it.

We conclude this book by focusing on learning, which we argue is the very core of Prepared Leadership. Because without learning before, during, and after a crisis—without doing the work, asking the questions, reflecting on the experience, and capturing and acting on the lessons—we are destined to fall once again into the cycles of panic and neglect that leave us vulnerable to the next crisis and the one after that.

This book provides you with a framework, with insights and techniques as well as examples and with tools from our research, that we hope will help *you* become a Prepared Leader. Above all, we hope this book gives you hope and a sense of optimism that you have the agency and the wherewithal to shape outcomes and lead yourself and your organization forward, whatever the future holds.

Optimism is a keyword. For both of us, weathering the storms of the pandemic era as new leaders has been enormously testing. We both took up historic appointments at the helm of renowned institutions, even as COVID-19 was closing campuses and spreading uncertainty all over the world. Leading through this period was at times harrowing. Among the many lessons that this crisis has taught us is the need to find balance—that you cannot divorce yourself and your personal circumstances from the reality of being a leader that other people look to and need for guidance.

This has been challenging but also an opportunity for learning and growth. Balancing empathy with accountability, giving hope that things will get better while dealing with extraordinary uncertainty, leading in the weeds but knowing when to focus on the demands of strategic leadership—all of this has called for the endless support of our colleagues, our teams, and our closest friends and family—our *personal* boards of directors.

We have both come to understand that as leaders, we are not immune to the stresses and the strain that come with a crisis of this magnitude. Coping as people, as human beings, has meant finding joy amid anxiety and uncertainty. For us, this has meant surrounding ourselves with those close enough to see us at our worst, at our least certain—those people who have our best interests at heart, who have helped us do this hard work, and who have supported us tirelessly as we were on stage, on call, on deck and on duty throughout this crisis. It has meant finding time for family, culture, and repose—and time to connect with our colleagues over a meal, as human beings. Finding the strength to lead has also meant drawing on our broader skill set as parents and tapping into a kind of muscle memory that has helped us nurture others and give them hope even if, at times, we haven't felt much hope ourselves.

Writing this book has given us great optimism. It has been and will continue to be a guide for us both as leaders at a time of great crisis. *The Prepared Leader* captures our many years of research, our evolved thinking, and our lived experience as scholars and leaders. It has enabled us to articulate our own learning during this crisis and to shape that learning into a framework that we, too, have used throughout the pandemic era.

Ahead of us remain many challenges and crises yet to take shape. For Erika, there is the imperative to innovate and to keep pace with the needs, goals, and values of the next generation of leaders. That will mean leveraging many of the lessons that the pandemic has had to share about health equity; diversity and inclusion; and environmental, social, and corporate governance, to build out a curricular offering in business education that is fit for future purposes. Erika hopes "The Wharton Way" will become the end vision of this imperative.

For Lynn, it means fulfilling the vision that John Simmons articulated 125 years ago and planting a flag for education as a vehicle for equity and empowerment in 2022 and beyond. For us both, rising to the challenges of what's next, bracing for change, and preparing for the unknown and unexpected is very much about following the precepts of Prepared Leadership. It means scanning our environment, analyzing the horizon, surrounding ourselves with the right people, and asking the right questions—chief among them, what did I learn?

The Prepared Leader functions as a guide and as a reference for us as we look forward to what's next. As well, it is a reminder to lead by example. We hope it will do the same for you.

Acknowledgments

We began this project before COVID-19 was on the radar screen for the United States and before either of us was in a search process for our respective roles as dean of the Wharton School or president of Simmons University. Accordingly, our intention was to fully author *The Prepared Leader* ourselves. When the pandemic hit at the same time we assumed two significant and visible leadership roles in higher education, we knew two things: First, this moment in time was too important for us not to capture through the book, given our crisis leadership expertise. Second, the demands of our new jobs would preclude us from completing the project ourselves.

Aine Doris has been an extraordinary collaborator in writing *The Prepared Leader*. Her keen intellect, research skills, and seemingly effortless writing style were just what we needed to keep us focused and on track. With her support, we are pleased to have produced a book that builds on our years of research, is positioned within a contemporary context, and highlights the issues of the times.

Barbara Demarest has been a long-time partner in helping us translate our ideas into graphic form and in the preparation of learning tools found throughout this book and that form the essence of www.jamesandwooten.com.

Clearly, our leadership at the Wharton School and Simmons University amid crisis and societal unrest has provided ample opportunity for us to demonstrate prepared leadership. We have not been perfect leaders, but we have been guided by the principles of this book and are grateful to our colleagues, students, and alumni, who have displayed incredible patience and trust in us.

We are grateful to Angela Bostick, Chief Marketing and Communications Officer at the Wharton School, for her steadfast support in our commitment to publish *The Prepared Leader* with Wharton School Press (WSP). At WSP, Shannon Berning and Brett LoGiurato have been a marvelous editorial team. Thank you for your expert opinion and guidance through the details of the manuscript preparation.

Several universities have played particularly important roles in our development as academics and crisis leaders. Emory and Cornell universities were the schools where we each initially tested our leadership skill when the pandemic first surfaced. We are grateful to our leadership teams, who worked tirelessly with us as we navigated through the early days of the pandemic. And finally, we were both trained at the University of Michigan. Our career trajectories were catapulted from this incredible launching pad, and the research skills we gained while doctoral students there have shaped our work as crisis leadership scholars ever since.

Notes

1   Tedros Adhanom Ghebreyesus, "WHO Director-General's Opening Remarks at the Media Briefing on COVID-19," World Health Organization, March 11, 2020, https://www.who.int/director-general/speeches/detail/who-director-general-s -opening-remarks-at-the-media-briefing-on-COVID-19---11-march-2020.

2   Eduardo Levy Yeyati and Federico Filippini, "Social and Economic Impact of COVID-19" (Brookings Global Working Paper #158, June 2021), https://www .brookings.edu/wp-content/uploads/2021/06/Social-and-economic-impact -COVID.pdf.

3   The World Bank, "COVID-19 to Add as Many as 150 Million Extreme Poor by 2021," press release, October 7, 2020, https://www.worldbank.org/en/news/press -release/2020/10/07/covid-19-to-add-as-many-as-150-million-extreme-poor-by -2021.

4   International Labor Organization, "COVID-19 and the World of Work, Seventh Edition: Updated Estimates and Analysis," *ILO Monitor*, January 25, 2021, https://www.ilo.org/wcmsp5/groups/public/@dgreports/@dcomm/documents /briefingnote/wcms_767028.pdf.

5   Joshua Lederberg, "Medical Science, Infectious Disease, and the Unity of Humanity," *Journal of the American Medical Association* 160, no. 5 (August 5, 1988): 684–685, https://jamanetwork.com/journals/jama/article-abstract /373248.

6   Robin Marantz Henig, "Experts Warned of a Pandemic Decades Ago. Why Weren't We Ready?" *National Geographic Magazine*, April 8, 2020, https://www .nationalgeographic.com/science/2020/04/experts-warned-pandemic-decades -ago-why-not-ready-for-coronavirus/#close.

7   James Palsey, "How SARS Terrified the World in 2003, Infecting More Than 8,000 People and Killing 774," *Business Insider*, February 21, 2020, https://www .businessinsider.com/deadly-sars-virus-history-2003-in-photos-2020-2.

8   Bill Gates, "How to Fight the Next Epidemic," *New York Times*, March 18, 2015, https://www.nytimes.com/2015/03/18/opinion/bill-gates-the-ebola-crisis-was -terrible-but-next-time-could-be-much-worse.html.

9   Sophie Edwards, "Pandemic Response a Cycle of 'Panic and Neglect,' Says World Bank President," *Devex*, April 5, 2017, https://www.devex.com/news/pandemic -response-a-cycle-of-panic-and-neglect-says-world-bank-president-89995.

10 For more, see the following sources: J. G. March and H. A. Simon, *Organizations* (New York: Wiley, 1958); Max H. Bazerman, *Judgment in Managerial Decision Making*, 4th ed. (New York: John Wiley & Sons, 1998); Max H. Bazerman and Dolly Chugh, "Bounded Awareness: Focusing Failures in Negotiation," in *Negotiation Theory and Research*, ed. L. Thompson (New York: Psychological Press, 2006); Max H. Bazerman and Dolly Chugh, "Decisions without Blinders," *Harvard Business Review 84*, no. 1 (2006): 88–97, https://hbr.org/2006/01 /decisions-without-blinders; Max H. Bazerman and Michael D. Watkins, *Predictable Surprises* (Boston: Harvard Business School Press, 2003); Amos Tversky and Daniel Kahneman, "Judgment under Uncertainty: Heuristics and Biases," *Science* 211 (1974): 453–463, https://www.science.org/doi/10.1126 /science.185.4157.1124; and A. Tversky and D. Kahneman, "Advances in Prospect Theory: Cumulative Representation of Uncertainty," *Journal of Risk and Uncertainty* 5 (1992): 297–323, https://www.jstor.org/stable/41755005.

11 Toby Helm, Emma Graham-Watson, and Robin McKie, "How Did Britain Get Its COVID Response So Wrong?" *The Guardian*, April 19, 2020, https://www .theguardian.com/world/2020/apr/18/how-did-britain-get-its-response-to -coronavirus-so-wrong.

12 Dan Woike, "Adam Silver Says NBA Is Prepared to Change Plans If Coronavirus Protocols Fail," *Los Angeles Times*, December 21, 2020, https://www.latimes.com /sports/story/2020-12-21/adam-silver-coronavirus-problems-nba-season.

13 Adrian Wojnarowski and Zach Lowe, "NBA Revenue for 2019–2020 Dropped 10% to $8.3 Billion, Sources Say," ESPN.com, October 28, 2020, https://www .espn.com/nba/story/_/id/30211678/nba-revenue-2019-20-season-dropped-10-83 -billion-sources-say.

14 Michaela J. Kerrissy and Amy C. Edmondson, "What Good Leadership Looks Like During This Pandemic," *Harvard Business Review*, April 13, 2020, https://hbr .org/2020/04/what-good-leadership-looks-like-during-this-pandemic.

15 Erika Hayes James and Lynn Perry Wooten, https://jamesandwooten.com/.

16 Helen Macdonald, "The Mysterious Lives of Birds Who Never Come Down," *New York Times*, July 29, 2020, https://www.nytimes.com/2020/07/29/magazine /vesper-flights.html.

17 Macdonald, "The Mysterious Lives of Birds."

18 Erika Hayes James and Lynn Perry Wooten, https://jamesandwooten.com/. See Christine M. Pearson and Judith A. Clair, "Reframing Crisis Management," *Academy of Management Review* 23, no. 1 (1998): 59–76; and Christine M. Pearson and Ian I. Mitroff, "From Crisis Prone to Crisis Prepared: A Framework for Crisis Management," *Academy of Management Executive* 7, no. 1 (1993): 48–58.

19 Jan Schwartz, "Volkswagen Managers Were Notified About Diesel Probe in May 2014," *Reuters*, February 16, 2016, https://www.reuters.com/article /volkswagen-emissions/volkswagen-managers-were-notified-about-diesel-probe -in-may-2014-sources-idUSL2N15V0IL.

20 Natasha Frost, "Battling Delta, New Zealand Abandons Zero-COVID
Ambitions," *New York Times*, October 4, 2021, https://www.nytimes.com/2021
/10/04/world/australia/new-zealand-covid-zero.html.

21 Rob Davies, "JD Wetherspoons Denies 'Abandoning' Staff in Coronavirus
Crisis," *The Guardian*, March 24, 2020, https://www.theguardian.com/business
/2020/mar/24/wetherspoons-denies-abandoning-staff-in-coronavirus-crisis.

22 Phil Simon, "How Nextdoor Addressed Racial Profiling on Its Platform,"
Harvard Business Review, May 11, 2018, https://hbr.org/2018/05/how-nextdoor
-addressed-racial-profiling-on-its-platform.

23 James and Wooten, https://jamesandwooten.com/.

24 Kristin Stoller, "Mercury Systems, Zoom and DocuSign CEOs Are Among the
Highest-Rated Business Leaders During the COVID-19 Crisis," *Forbes*,
September 16, 2020, https://www.forbes.com/sites/kristinstoller/2020/09/16
/mercury-systems-zoom-and-docusign-ceos-are-among-the-highest-rated
-business-leaders-during-the-covid-19-crisis/?sh=40373b0341f4.

25 Jason C. W. Hancock, "Mark Aslett: Kindness, Empathy and Compassion as
Business Imperatives: A Q&A with the CEO of Mercury Systems," *SpencerStuart*
(November 2020), https://www.spencerstuart.com/research-and-insight
/kindness-empathy-and-compassion-as-business-imperatives.

26 Hancock, "Mark Aslett."

27 Erika Hayes James and Lynn Perry Wooten, https://jamesandwooten.com/. See
Erika H. James and Lynn Perry Wooten, "Leadership as (Un)usual: How to
Display Competence in Times of Crisis," *Organizational Dynamics* 34, no. 2
(2005): 141–152; and Lynn Perry Wooten and Erika H. James, "Linking Crisis
Management and Leadership Competencies: The Role of Human Resource
Development," *Advances in Developing Human Resources* 10, no. 3 (2008):
352–379, https://doi.org/10.1177/1523422308316450.

28 James and Wooten, https://jamesandwooten.com/.

29 Hancock, "Mark Aslett."

30 Jeff Zillgitt, "How NBA Commissioner Adam Silver's Decision May Have Slowed
Coronavirus Spread in Sports," *USA Today*, March 18, 2020, https://www
.usatoday.com/story/sports/nba/2020/03/18/nba-adam-silver-may-have-saved
-sports-coronavirus/5062457002/.

31 John Kotter, "Should NBA Commissioner Adam Silver Be Our Country's
COVID-19 Czar?" *Forbes*, October 27, 2020, https://www.forbes.com/sites
/johnkotter/2020/10/27/should-nba-commissioner-adam-silver-be-our-countrys
-covid-19-czar/?sh=38c97fff5010.

32 Hancock, "Mark Aslett."

33 Dan Wetzel, "Why NBA Commissioner Adam Silver's Coronavirus Response
Was the Wakeup Call America Needed," *Yahoo! Sports*, March 14, 2020,

https://www.yahoo.com/video/why-nba-commissioner-adam-silvers
-coronavirus-response-was-the-wakeup-call-america-needed-163655390.html.

34   Ron Ruggless, "One Year in, COVID-19 Pandemic Continues to Impact
Independent Restaurants," *Restaurant Hospitality,* March 15, 2021, https://www
.restaurant-hospitality.com/operations/one-year-covid-19-pandemic-continues
-impact-independent-restaurants.

35   Alicia Kelso, "Burger King Unveils New Restaurant Design Shaped by the Age of
COVID-19," *Forbes,* September 3, 2020, https://www.forbes.com/sites/aliciakelso
/2020/09/03/burger-king-unveils-a-new-restaurant-design-to-meet-consumer
-habits-changed-by-covid-19/?sh=722376542b15.

36   Kabir Ahuja, Vishwa Chandra, Victoria Lord, and Curtis Preens, "Ordering in:
The Rapid Evolution of Food Delivery," McKinsey and Company, September 22,
2021, https://www.mckinsey.com/industries/technology-media-and
-telecommunications/our-insights/ordering-in-the-rapid-evolution-of-food
-delivery.

37   See, for example, Lee G. Bolman and Terrence E. Deal, *Reframing Organizations:
Artistry, Choice, and Leadership* (San Francisco, CA: Jossey-Bass, 2013).

38   Robert E. Quinn, "Moments of Greatness: Entering the Fundamental State of
Leadership," *Harvard Business Review,* July–August 2005, https://hbr.org/2005
/07/moments-of-greatness-entering-the-fundamental-state-of-leadership.

39   For more on these biases, check out resources at https://thedecisionlab.com/
biases.

40   Alex Pentland, "Beyond the Echo Chamber," *Harvard Business Review* 91
(November 2013): 80–86.

41   For more on the confirming effect, see the resources at https://thedecisionlab.
com/biases/confirmation-bias.

42   Paul Holmes, Arun Sudhamen, and Aarti Shah, "Crisis Review: The Top 20
Crises of 2020 (Part 1 of 3)," PRovoke Media, https://www.provokemedia.com
/long-reads/article/crisis-review-the-top-20-crises-of-2020-(part-1-of-3).

43   Restaurant Brands International, "An Open Letter from the CEO of Restaurant
Brands International:" https://www.prnewswire.com/news-releases/an-open
-letter-from-the-ceo-of-restaurant-brands-international-301032012.html.

44   Mark Turner, interviewed by the authors, October 12, 2020. All subsequent
quotes from Turner are from the same interview.

45   Wonya Lucas, interviewed by the authors, October 26, 2020. All subsequent
quotes from Lucas are from the same interview.

46   See, for example, John J. Gabarro, *The Dynamics of Taking Charge* (Brighton,
MA: Harvard Business Publishing, 1987); Diego Gambetta, "Trust: Making and
Breaking Cooperative Relations," *British Journal of Sociology* 13, no. 1; and Roy
Lewicki and Barbara Bunker, "Trust in Relationships: A Model of Development
and Decline," in *Conflict Cooperation and Justice: Essays Inspired by the Work of*

Morton Deutsch, ed. Barbara B. Bunker and Jeffrey Z. Rubin (San Francisco, CA: Jossey-Bass, 1995), 133–173. See also, for example, the work of Bernard Barber, *The Logic and Limits of Trust* (Rutgers, NJ: Rutgers University Press, 1983); or Niklas Luhman, "Familiarity, Confidence, Trust: Problems and Alternatives," in *Making and Breaking Cooperative Relations*, ed. Diego Gambetta (Oxford: University of Oxford Press, 2000), 94–107. See the Russell Sage Foundation website for more information and a complete listing of the work they have produced on trust: https://www.russellsage.org/publications/books/subjects /TRUST. And see Dennis S. Reina and Michelle L Reina, *Trust and Betrayal in the Workplace: Building Effective Relationships in Your Organization* (Oakland, CA: Berrett-Koehler, 2015).

47 Darden Business Publishing cases are copyrighted by the University of Virginia Darden School Foundation, Charlottesville, VA. All rights reserved. No part of this publication may be reproduced, stored in a retrieval system, used in a spreadsheet, or transmitted in any form or by any means—electronic, mechanical, photocopying, recording, or otherwise—without the written permission of the Darden School Foundation.

48 Debra Meyerson, Karl E. Weick, and Roderick M. Kramer, "Swift Trust in Temporary Groups," in *Trust in Organizations: Frontiers of Theory and Research*, ed. Roderick Kramer and Tom Tyler (Thousand Oaks, CA: SAGE, 1996), 166–195.

49 Henri Lipmanowicz and Keith McCandless, *The Surprising Power of Liberating Structures: Simple Rules to Unleash a Culture of Innovation* (Seattle: Liberating Structures Press, 2015).

50 For more, see Robert B. Archibald and David H. Feldman, *Why Does College Cost So Much?* (Oxford University Press, 2010); and Tyrone McKinley Freeman and A'Lelia Bundles, *Madam C. J. Walker's Gospel of Giving: Black Women's Philanthropy During Jim Crow* (University of Illinois Press, 2020).

51 Branko Milanovic, "The First Global Event in the History of Humankind," *Social Europe*, December 7, 2020, https://socialeurope.eu/the-first-global-event -in-the-history-of-humankind.

52 Edward Wong and Steven Lee Myers, "Officials Push U.S.-China Relations Toward Point of No Return," *New York Times*, December 8, 2020, https://www .nytimes.com/2020/07/25/world/asia/us-china-trump-xi.html.

53 Provoke Media, "Crisis Review: The Top 20 Crises of 2020 (Part 3 of 3)," February 1, 2021, https://www.provokemedia.com/long-reads/article/crisis -review-the-top-20-crises-of-2020-(part-3-of-3).

54 Gillian Friedman, "Here's What Companies Are Promising to Do to Fight Racism," *New York Times*, August 23, 2020, https://www.nytimes.com/article /companies-racism-george-floyd-protests.html; and Tracy Jan, Jena McGregor, and Meghan Hoyer, "Corporate America's $50 Billion Promise," *Washington Post*, August 23, 2021, https://www.washingtonpost.com/business/interactive /2021/george-floyd-corporate-america-racial-justice/.

55   Provoke Media, "Crisis Review."

56   See, for example, Orly Levy, Schon Beechler, Sully Taylor, and Nakiye A. Boyacigiller, "What We Talk About When We Talk About 'Global Mindset': Managerial Cognition in Multinational Corporations," *Journal of International Business Studies* 38, no. 2 (2007): 231–258, http://www.jstor.org/stable/4540418; and Levy, et al., "Global Mindset: A Review and Proposed Extensions," in *Advances in International Management: The Global Mindset*, ed. M. Javidan, R. M. Steers, and M. A. Hitt (Oxford: Elsevier), 11–47.

57   See Hofstede Insights, "National Culture," n.d., https://hi.hofstede-insights.com /national-culture.

58   Sama Kubba, "The Importance of Culture in Societal Responses to COVID-19," *Harvard Political Review*, October 14, 2020, https://harvardpolitics.com/culture -response-covid-19/.

59   See, for example, Deloitte, "A Call for Accountability and Action: The Deloitte Global 2021 Millennial and Gen Z Survey," 2021, https://www2.deloitte.com /content/dam/Deloitte/global/Documents/2021-deloitte-global-millennial -survey-report.pdf; and Kubba, "The Importance of Culture." See also, National League of Cities, "Three Ways COVID-19 Impacts Millennials Differently Than Boomers," n.d., https://www.nlc.org/article/2020/10/06/three-ways-COVID-19 -impacts-millennials-differently-than-boomers/.

60   Avivah Wittenberg-Cox and Tomas Chamorro-Premuzic, "Will the Pandemic Reshape Notions of Female Leadership?" *Harvard Business Review*, June 26, 2020, https://hbr.org/2020/06/will-the-pandemic-reshape-notions-of-female -leadership.

61   Jack Zenger and Joseph Folkman, "Research: Women Are Better Leaders During a Crisis," *Harvard Business Review*, December 30, 2020, https://hbr.org/2020/12 /research-women-are-better-leaders-during-a-crisis.

62   Nina Goswami, "Have Female CEOs Coped Better with COVID Than Men?" BBC, November 19, 2020, https://www.bbc.com/news/business-54974132.

63   Wonya Lucas, interviewed by the authors, October 26, 2020.

64   Erika Hayes James and Lynn Perry Wooten, *Leading Under Pressure: From Surviving to Thriving Before, During and After a Crisis* (New York: Routledge, 2010). See also Gerencser, Mark, Reginald Van Lee, Fernando Napolitano, and Christopher Kelly, *Megacommunities: How Leaders of Government, Business and Non-Profits Can Tackle Today's Global Challenges Together* (New York: Palgrave MacMillan, 2008).

65   See Erika Hayes James and Lynn Perry Wooten, "Sexual Harassment in the Workplace: A Risk Without Equal," white paper, https://www.emorybusiness .com/wp-content/uploads/2018/04/EmoryCornell_180426.pdf.

66   Michael Lepage, "First Pfizer/BioNTech Coronavirus Vaccinations Take Place in the UK," *New Scientist*, December 8, 2020, https://www.newscientist.com/article /2262085-first-pfizer-biontech-coronavirus-vaccinations-take-place-in-the-uk/.

67 Mark Turner, interviewed by the authors, October 12, 2020. All subsequent quotes from Turner are from the same interview.

68 "COVIDview Summary Ending on . . . ," Center for Disease Control and Prevention, https://www.cdc.gov/coronavirus/2019-ncov/COVID-data /COVIDview/past-reports/06262020.html, updated weekly.

69 Ryan Brooks and David Mack, "The Head of CrossFit Has Stepped Down After Telling Staff on a Zoom Call, 'We're Not Mourning for George Floyd,'" *BuzzFeed News*, June 9, 2020, https://www.buzzfeednews.com/article/ryancbrooks/crossfit -ceo-founder-zoom-greg-glassman-george-floyd.

70 Joe Genetin-Pilawa, "Glassman to Nine-Year Affiliate Owner 'You Are Delusional,'" *Morning Chalk Up*, June 7, 2020, https://morningchalkup.com /2020/06/07/glassman-to-nine-year-affiliate-owner-you-are-delusional/.

71 The tool can be found on the authors' website, https://jamesandwooten.com/wp -content/uploads/2020/07/4-socialmedia.pdf.

72 See, for example, Paula Bellostas Muguerza, Johanna Tybus, and Carsten Passlick, "A COVID-19-led Healthcare Digital Transformation," Kearney, n.d., https://www.kearney.com/health/article?/a/a-COVID-19-led-healthcare-digital -transformation.

73 Mauro Guillén, interviewed by the authors on January 19, 2020.

74 Lubomila Jordanova, interviewed by the authors on February 3, 2020. All subsequent quotes from Jordanova are from the same interview.

75 Swiss Re Group, "Global Insured Catastrophe Losses Rise to USD 112 Billion in 2021, the Fourth Highest on Record, Swiss Re Institute Estimates," press release, December 14, 2021, https://www.swissre.com/media/news-releases/nr-20211214 -sigma-full-year-2021-preliminary-natcat-loss-estimates.html.

76 See "Working During the COVID-19 Pandemic: Class Differences," JobList, February 28, 2021, https://www.joblist.com/trends/working-during-the-COVID-19 -pandemic-class-differences.

77 Ian Begley, "Adam Silver: NBA to Review Policies," ESPN, September 22, 2014, https://www.espn.com/nba/story/_/id/11570243/adam-silver-says-nba-evaluate -disciplinary-policies.

78 See Darin Gantt, "NBA Nails It on Domestic Violence Ruling While NFL Struggles," NBC Sports, November 20, 2014, https://profootballtalk.nbcsports .com/2014/11/20/nba-nails-it-on-domestic-violence-ruling-while-nfl-struggles/.

79 NBA Communications, "Adam Silver's Statement Regarding Hornets' Jeffrey Taylor," November 19, 2014, https://pr.nba.com/jeffery-taylor-adam-silver -statement.

80 Brandon Gomez, "CrossFit Gym Chain Caught up in LGBTQ Rights Controversy, Religious Friction," CNBC, June 7, 2018, https://www.cnbc.com /2018/06/07/gym-chain-crossfit-caught-up-in-lgbtq-rights-controversy .html.

81   Katherine Rosman, "CrossFit Owner Fostered Sexist Company Culture, Workers Say," *New York Times*, June 20, 2020, https://www.nytimes.com/2020 /06/20/style/greg-glassman-crossfit-sexism.html.

82   See Noah Manskar, "Ex-CrossFit CEO Greg Glassman Accused of Mistreating Women," *New York Post*, June 16, 2020, https://nypost.com/2020/06/16/andy -stumpf-accuses-greg-glassman-of-harassment-at-crossfit/.

83   Erika Hayes James and Lynn Perry Wooten, *Leading Under Pressure: From Surviving to Thriving Before, During and After a Crisis* (New York: Routledge, 2010).

84   Kristy Towry, Willie Choi, Gary Hecht, and Ivo Tafkov interviewed by the authors on February 12, 2021. All other quotes by Towry, Hecht, et al. from the same interview.

85   Erika Hayes James and Lynn Perry Wooten, https://jamesandwooten.com/.

Index

Note: Page numbers in italics indicate figures or tables.

About the Authors

Erika H. James became the dean of the Wharton School on July 1, 2020. Trained as an organizational psychologist, James is a leading expert on crisis leadership, workplace diversity, and management strategy, and is coauthor of *The Prepared Leader: Emerge from Any Crisis More Resilient Than Before.*

Prior to her appointment at Wharton, James was the John H. Harland Dean at Emory University's Goizueta Business School from 2014 to 2020.

An award-winning educator, accomplished consultant, and researcher, she is the first woman and first person of color to be appointed dean in Wharton's 139-year history. As such, she has paved the way for women in leadership, both in education and corporate America. James has been instrumental in developing groundbreaking executive education programs and in advising companies across various industries on their diversity and crisis leadership strategies.

Known internationally, James was named as one of the "Top 10 Women of Power in Education" by *Black Enterprise* and as one of the "Power 100" by *Ebony*. She has been quoted as an expert thought leader by the *Wall Street Journal*, MSNBC, CNN.com, and numerous other media outlets.

In addition to her academic responsibilities, James is a board member of Morgan Stanley and SurveyMonkey, a California-based market research and customer-experience company, and several organizations that align with her passion for education and advancing women in business.

James holds a PhD and a master's degree in organizational psychology from the University of Michigan, as well as a bachelor's degree in psychology from Pomona College of the Claremont Colleges in California.

Lynn Perry Wooten, coauthor of *The Prepared Leader: Emerge from Any Crisis More Resilient Than Before*, a seasoned academic and an expert on organizational development and transformation, became the ninth president of Simmons University on July 1, 2020. She is the first African American to lead the university.

Specializing in crisis leadership, diversity and inclusion, and positive leadership—organizational behavior that reveals and nurtures the highest level of human potential—Wooten is an innovative leader and prolific author and presenter whose research has informed her work in the classroom and as an administrator. She first joined a university faculty in 1994 and has served in administrative roles since 2008. Wooten came to Simmons from Cornell University, where she was the David J. Nolan Dean and Professor of Management and Organizations at the Dyson School of Applied Economics and Management.

Wooten has also had a robust clinical practice, providing leadership development, education, and training for a wide variety of companies and institutions, from the Kellogg Foundation to Harvard University's Kennedy School, to Google.

With leadership at the core of her work, Wooten's research has ranged from an NIH-funded investigation of how leadership can positively alleviate health disparities, to leading in a crisis and managing workforce diversity. In addition to *The Prepared Leader* (Wharton School Press), she is the coauthor of *Arrive and Thrive: 7 Impactful Practices for Women Navigating Leadership* (2022) and the coeditor of *Positive Organizing in a Global Society: Understanding and Engaging Differences for Capacity Building and Inclusion* (2016). Sharing her work at nearly 60 symposia and conferences, she also is the author of nearly 30 journal articles and more than 15 book chapters, as well as managerial monographs and numerous teaching cases.

Wooten holds a PhD in corporate strategy from the University of Michigan, an MBA from Duke University's Fuqua School of Business, and a Bachelor of Science in accounting from North Carolina A&T State University.

For more research and insights from James and Wooten, please visit jamesandwooten.com.

**WHARTON
SCHOOL
PRESS**

About Wharton School Press

Wharton School Press, the book publishing arm of the Wharton School of the University of Pennsylvania, was established to inspire bold, insightful thinking within the global business community.

Wharton School Press publishes a select list of award-winning, bestselling, and thought-leading books that offer trusted business knowledge to help leaders at all levels meet the challenges of today and the opportunities of tomorrow. Led by a spirit of innovation and experimentation, Wharton School Press leverages groundbreaking digital technologies and has pioneered a fast-reading business book format that fits readers' busy lives, allowing them to swiftly emerge with the tools and information needed to make an impact. Wharton School Press books offer guidance and inspiration on a variety of topics, including leadership, management, strategy, innovation, entrepreneurship, finance, marketing, social impact, public policy, and more.

Wharton School Press also operates an online bookstore featuring a curated selection of influential books by Wharton School faculty and Press authors, published by a wide range of leading publishers.

To find books that will inspire and empower you to increase your impact and expand your personal and professional horizons, visit *wsp.wharton.upenn.edu.*

Wharton
UNIVERSITY of PENNSYLVANIA

About the Wharton School

Founded in 1881 as the world's first collegiate business school, the Wharton School of the University of Pennsylvania is shaping the future of business by incubating ideas, driving insights, and creating leaders who change the world. With a faculty of more than 235 renowned professors, Wharton has 5,000 undergraduate, MBA, executive MBA, and doctoral students. Each year 13,000 professionals from around the world advance their careers through Wharton Executive Education's individual, company-customized, and online programs. More than 100,000 Wharton alumni form a powerful global network of leaders who transform business every day.

www.wharton.upenn.edu

CPSIA information can be obtained
at www.ICGtesting.com
Printed in the USA
JSHW052147171022
31787JS00005B/5